DETERMINED TO ESCAPE

DETERMINED TO ESCAPE

BEVERLEE HILTON

XULON PRESS

Xulon Press
2301 Lucien Way #415
Maitland, FL 32751
407.339.4217
www.xulonpress.com

© 2022 by Beverlee Hilton

All rights reserved solely by the author. The author guarantees all contents are original and do not infringe upon the legal rights of any other person or work. No part of this book may be reproduced in any form without the permission of the author.

Due to the changing nature of the Internet, if there are any web addresses, links, or URLs included in this manuscript, these may have been altered and may no longer be accessible. The views and opinions shared in this book belong solely to the author and do not necessarily reflect those of the publisher. The publisher therefore disclaims responsibility for the views or opinions expressed within the work.

Unless otherwise indicated, Scripture quotations taken from the King James Version (KJV) – *public domain*.

Paperback ISBN-13: 978-1-6628-5085-1
Ebook ISBN-13: 978-1-6628-5086-8

Table of Contents

Introduction vii

Chapter 1   Divorced Mother 1
Chapter 2   Call them Mom and Pop 5
Chapter 3   Afghanistan 27
Chapter 4   The Silent Prayer 43
Chapter 5   Rainy Days 51
Chapter 6   The Boyfriend 63
Chapter 7   The Sentence 71
Chapter 8   St. Rose 81
Chapter 9   A Breath of Fresh Air 95
Chapter 10   Hillcrest School for Girls 99
Chapter 11   The Freedom Building 115
Chapter 12   Don't Turn Around 129
Chapter 13   The Marriage I Dreamed About 133
Chapter 14   My Best Decision 153
Chapter 15   Antics of Harry, Mothers Childhood 161

Mother's Childhood 165

Introduction

Take anyone's family in the world, separate them, have them write about what happened in their household, and each story would be different.

We are individuals. We think different and feel different. Some people are strong and courageous, while others are shy and introverted. God didn't make us all the same, as He didn't make us all the same color.

This story is about a young married couple in the late 1940s and 50s; how they strove to make a family unit, while they searched for employment and raised two very young girls. Once divorced, the wife Doris and new husband Harry depended on Harry's parents in many ways, and at times, the youngsters were left in their care at their farm in Oregon.

As time went on, they would travel together in trailers with relatives from place to place, working for lumber companies. The girls and their cousins went to several different schools in a year. During the months that lumber companies were idle, the families returned to Dexter.

The couple grew apart when Harry became seriously ill with tuberculosis and was hospitalized. The entire family struggled in their separate directions, as their own personalities grew stronger.

Divorce, again, was inevitable, but Harry's diagnosis of another disease would bring them back together. The youngest rebelled at the reunion and concluded it would be better to leave then stay in the dysfunctional home. Her trials of "finding her way" took her to three different detention homes while she learned several lessons of life. Her trials would eventually bring her to salvation, which she "thought" she already had. In depression, she sought God with her whole heart, and that's where the answer was.

Chapter 1
Divorced Mother

On a cool spring day in April 1946, I breathed my first breath of life. The war was over, and my parents moved back to South Dakota, where my dad, Roger's, parents lived. Mother had lived in California while awaiting Roger's return from his hitch in the Navy in Hawaii. She had worked in a factory there, helping with the "nuts and bolts" for the airplanes while the war was going on, and Barbara, my sister, was born in 1942 while she was there.

I'm afraid it must have been a tumultuous time for my mother, at the age of twenty-three, going through a divorce and planning to take me and four-year-old Barbara to Oregon to live with some of her family. She had received an injection to induce labor a week before I was born because she was in major stress with the divorce. It was unknown to her at that moment that her father would pass away that week. She expressed to me several years later that her decision for the inducement probably saved my life. She felt sure that if she had waited for my birth, which was thought to be end of April, she would have lost me from heartbreak, as her father died on my scheduled day of arrival.

Fritz, had suffered a stroke from working in the field, and he had been her sole help in raising Barbara at that point. She left me in the hospital for about ten days, she said, until she was able to care for me. Now divorced and fatherless, she, Barb, and I caught a train to Pendleton, Oregon, where her mother lived, and she could help her until she got on her feet. Grandma Rosa had divorced Fritz several years prior. I was never told the reason why. I believe the Depression was one reason. Fritz had been in a cattle business and lost most of their savings and the cattle.

Mother said she had no money to buy us food for the train trip. She told me about the man at the train station who was eating doughnuts and that Barb stared at him every bite he took. Mother said she felt sad but encouraged herself in thinking things would get better when we got to Oregon.

On the train, we met two nuns who gladly helped watch over Barb and me until we reached Pendleton. They had mentioned they didn't realize a baby was on board because she had been so quiet.

We lived in Pendleton for several months, then moved to Portland to live with Mother's sister, Evelyn, a single woman in her thirties. We stayed with her several months. I don't recall those years, but these are the things I was told. Aunt Evelyn had no furniture for a baby, so at night, they put me in an old trunk they had. I was about two then, and Barbara six. I was told that I peeled the wallpaper while standing in the trunk.

After a while, Mothers' brother, Russ, introduced her to a friend of his, Harry Jr. Mr. Harry and Russ met at a bar where they frequented and became friends. They were working construction on the same job site in Cascade Locks and met after work to play pool. Mother then moved us to Cascade Locks, where Russ and Betty lived with their two kids, Guy, six, and Diana, four. Those were hard times, and a lot of people camped out, families all together, sometimes living in tents. Mother said one of the things she liked the most was what they called "hobo coffee," where you just put coffee in a can with water and heated it up by the fire. We ate many hot dogs and hard-boiled eggs, she said. Times were hard, but being with family helped in many ways. I don't know how the arrangement happened, but Barbara was sent to live with friends or relatives during that time. Boarding out children was not uncommon in those days.

Mother had tried to get a little money from Roger, but he had hired a lawyer and got out of it. I found out years later that my dad actually drove to Cascade Locks to ask Mother to come back to him. She refused, so he felt he shouldn't need to support us, seeing that Mr. Harry was a man very interested in her. Barbara, although very young, said she could remember Roger coming to visit in a fancy red convertible, and women standing around, admiring it. Roger's mother, my grandmother, Edina, sent money to us once in a while, on our birthdays and at Christmas. Mother and Edina stayed friends, with phone calls and mail for many years.

Uncle Russ and Harry's friendship were as close as brothers could be without being brothers. Harry's parents lived on a 600-acre parcel of farmland, where they raised chickens and cows. They had moved from Denver, Colorado, where they raised pigs, to Cascade Locks, along the Columbia River, then to a small town called Dexter, Oregon.

Chapter 2
Call them Mom and Pop

The farmhouse in Dexter was an old homestead. By that time, Mother and Harry had decided to marry. Harry called his mother and dad, Mom and Pop, so we called them that also. Mom had her heart set on Harry marrying a woman he had dated in Colorado, whom she had met and liked, and was not happy he had married a divorced woman with two small children. (Mom conveyed to me years later). In time, she softened and accepted us. It was a good thing because she took care of us girls for years, off and on, while Harry looked for construction jobs. He was a "powder monkey" and told many mischievous stories of his antics using dynamite as a teen.

Mother and Harry bought an old white twenty-five-foot trailer I remember well that had no inside bathroom. We lived in it a few years as we traveled from place to place, following the job sites with logging companies. When it rained hard, the ceiling leaked over Barb and my bunk beds. I was on the top bunk, so we had to share the bottom bunk until the rain stopped. We moved often. One year, we moved five times. As we traveled, Barb and I sang many songs, and sometimes we'd all sing. One of our favorites was, "You Are My Sunshine."

We went to many schools, and I remember how I hated my first days at new schools, although one of the schools wanted to put me up a grade higher than I was, because I had already learned what they were teaching. My parents said no, but many years later regretted it. Once, in the first grade, I remember Mother taking me to the school steps and giving me an ice cream to encourage me to stay. She said many times I'd just follow her back home.

I know times were hard, but as children, Barbara, our cousins, and I felt like nothing was unusual. We had each other and moved so often we had many new places to explore. Guy and Barb, being the oldest, were in charge of Diana and me most of the time. Our parents were gone several hours a day.

One winter while we were in Grants Pass, we decided to play "Billy Goats Gruff" on the small bridge that led into the trailer park where we were staying. We girls played the part on top of the bridge, and Guy played the "troll" underneath. There were just enough of us to play the game. I was the little goat, Diana was the middle goat, and Barb was the big Billy goat. We each took a turn at playing the troll. Eventually, we all ended up under the bridge playing on the frozen creek. We decided to walk on the ice and explore, to find out where it went and slip and slide around some. I remember seeing big bubbles under the ice and was wondering what made them. As I investigated, I slipped and fell part of the way in on the thin ice. Guy had been right next to me and grabbed me before I got more than my mittens wet. Then I was very cold, so we went back to the trailers.

Between jobs, we moved back to Dexter on Mom and Pop's farm. Look Out Point Dam was being built at that time, so, Pop had to let the government buy some of his land, for Highway 58 and Dexter Lake that was coming in on that property. The railroad bought some property of his on the other end, that split a parcel of land off by itself, where he had a few horses and some cattle. Trains came often rumbling by as we watched, and sometimes, we'd wave at the guy on the caboose and got thrilled if he waved back. Barbara, my cousins, and I explored the area and collected beautiful agates and sparkling rocks.

Pop had worked on the Hoover Dam in Denver until they laid him off. He had cabins that he rented to the men at the job site on his Dexter property. They had to move the cabins from where the lake would be coming through and up to the high end of his property. Also, there were two houses he had rented out, and they were moved also. One, we called "the yellow house." The other house we called "the white house."

Mom watched over Barb and me when we didn't go with our parents. We enjoyed the animals and were taught how to feed the cows. We watched Pop milk the two milk cows and learned how to feed them oats and grain. They were such gentle cows. They each had a calf every year, and the calves were friendly and loveable. They would gently lick my hand when I went to touch their nose. The bull was gentle also, and Pop let me sit on him awhile, but he had horns, and that was a little frightening to me.

One day, while Barb and I were playing in the barn, she decided we'd play cowboys, and I'd ride the cow. She found a rope and tied me to the calf so I wouldn't fall. The calf was fine until he spooked at something, and I slid under his belly, still tied. Somehow through my screaming and Barb's screaming, Pop showed up and rescued me. Both calf and I had escaped with no injuries. I think Barb got the switch that time.

I managed to get into some problems by myself also. I climbed up a tree and was afraid to come down, so Pop had to climb up and rescue me. I was after a bird's nest, where I managed to pull out two pretty blue eggs and accidentally crushed them, staining one of my socks before they hit the ground.

That same week, Barb decided we should play "You're the Cow, and I'm the Master." Guess who played the cow? So as a cow, I ate grass. I ate so much grass I got very sick and had to have an enema later that night. I learned not to eat grass, and Barbara was scolded. We didn't play that game anymore.

There was an old dog on the farm they called Coaly. He wasn't much fun to play with. I watched Mom put medicine on his tongue, and he'd just lie around. One day, I saw a new dog. He was so shy he wouldn't let us get near him. Mom called him Mischief. He disappeared one day, and we had another dog she called Fanny. Fanny was around a few years and had a litter or two, of adorable fuzzy puppies. She had the puppies under the house, where the wood stove was in the house. I just had to see them. I could hear them whimpering, so I crawled under the house toward the noises. It was a really tight fit. Fanny was tending gently with them. I tried to back out, but my jacket had hung up on a board, and I was stuck. I yelled out, and Pop had to crawl under the house and maneuver me back out. A few weeks later, Fanny brought those fuzzy little babies out.

I wanted one of my own, so I picked the one I wanted and named him Rinny, (after the famous Rin Tin Tin.) A friend of mine named Angeline took one of the other puppies. She lived in the trailer park behind the corner store and café, at the intersection of Dexter and Lost Creek Road. At that time, there was a little store, where us kids bought candy from the pop bottles, we collected in the trailer park.

There had been five puppies, and then there were only two. I asked Pop where the others were, and he said, "I knocked them in the head." When I realized what that meant, I was terribly angry because I had played with all of them, and had even taken some pictures. He said there were no homes for them to go to.

I found out, as time went on, that there were many things that happened on a farm that weren't pleasant. Butchering livestock was one, although, I had no problem with watching him take an ax and chop chickens' heads off. I understood the chickens and eggs were eatable, and I didn't have any chickens as pets. We didn't eat milk cows because they were for milk.

We found all kinds of things to do on the farm. Besides playing with the animals, we gathered eggs from the chicken house. Sometimes the hens would peck at us, and once a rooster chased us back to the house.

He ended up in the stock pot that next Sunday, made with dumplings. I was especially happy not to have to deal with him again.

In those days, we only had an outhouse. Being so young, I'm sure Barb and I had a "honey pot" under the bed, although I don't remember one. There was a bathtub in the kitchen behind the wood stove in a corner with a privacy screen we used once or twice a week.

Once I got into something that made me itch something awful. Mom washed me outside on the back porch in one of the big double sinks. Whatever it was I got into didn't happen again.

There were blackberry bushes all over the farm. We picked buckets and buckets of them. Mom made the best pies ever. She taught Barb how to bake, but I wasn't interested in the baking part. She made homemade noodles and had them on the counter behind the wood cooking stove to dry. I always found them and took a small handful, hoping she wouldn't notice. I watched her make butter and cottage cheese. That was interesting to me, especially the butter; it was so yellow. There were always pails of fresh milk that Pop brought to the back porch, strained and put in the cooler. There was no refrigerator, but the milk was always cool and delicious.

Mom always listened to Paul Harvey on the radio. I remember him because he always stated his name and ended his program with "Good day!" One of the songs I learned at that time was, "The Battle of New Orleans", Mom sang along with the radio. It must have been one of her favorites because she knew every word. She always seemed so cheery, singing or humming while she worked.

There were several apple trees that I enjoyed climbing and getting apples. One tree, in particular, had a perfect place for me to straddle, after I put my foot in one of the holes to climb up. I pretended it was a horse. I slowly got better at climbing them.

I rummaged around the old barn and found interesting things to play with. I found an old iron and pretended to iron imaginary clothes.

There were all kinds of treasures to play with, old buckets, dish pans, and good clean dirt. One of my favorite things was to play under the porch and make mud pies and decorate them with leaves. If I could find a flower or dandelion, I'd put it on my beautiful mud pie. I took egg shells out of the garbage and pretended to make breakfast, and fill the empty cans with more mud. I think I ate some of that dirt.

I preferred being outside with Pop working on fencing, or repairing some of the cabins they had around the place. Staying inside watching Mom sew on that old treadle sewing machine, was boring to me. Anything curtailing to outdoors was where I wanted to be. At that age, I didn't have to help with the dishes or clean the bedroom, just push my pajamas under the pillow. I did get to play house in one of the cabins that had a stove in it. I couldn't light it but it made my house-playing feel real. I gathered pots and pans from the old barn and busied myself for hours. I dressed one of the dogs up as my baby with an old dress I found, that probably at one time had been mine. I loved dressing the cats and dogs whenever they would let me.

Mom taught Barbara and I how to recite the Lord's Prayer. There was a picture of praying hands on the wall with the word's underneath. Every night we prayed, I always added that God would bring Charlie back home. Charlie was Harry's old horse he had for several years, now running loose on the thirty acres that were separated behind the railroad tracks. He told us the story of Charlie, and how he bought him from a fox farm that he had been working on. He was going to be slaughtered because he had injured his leg. He paid twenty dollars for him and nursed him back to health. I had decided I wanted that horse.

Sometimes, when we were snuggled into bed, under the warm comforter Mom made, she would let us listen to a few things on the radio. Roy Rogers and Dale Evens rescuing the good people or capturing the bad. The good guys always won. On rare occasions, we got to listen to *The Shadow Knows*. Mom wasn't one for telling bedtime stories. I was the story teller. I told a story that seemed to be one everyone remembered. It was about a crocodile that lived in the creek, and he was so big he ate the cars that traveled the road. I don't know how I came up with that story, but the adults had good laughs over it. My final line on the story was, "the people fell in the creek, and the alligator ate them." As we lulled off to sleep, we could hear the train clatter in the distance.

It seems like Pop and I never really finished a project; there were just so many things that had to be done. He was not the type to finish things; I guess he didn't want to get bored with any ones in particular. Mom scolded him about it daily, especially in the morning. She had a big bedroom downstairs with two big beds. Barb and I slept in one, and she in the other. Pop slept upstairs. She got up first in the morning, built a fire in the wood stove, and standing in front of it, put her corset on and got dressed. She made all her dresses. I never saw her in anything but a dress. She also made bib aprons to match her dresses. Those cold mornings, she'd holler. "Harrrryyyyyy, get up; get out of that bed." She must have said that hundreds of times in their married lives. I had heard it that much I think in the times I was living with them.

For breakfast, Mom always made soft-boiled eggs and oatmeal and homemade thick, sliced bread with butter and jam. To me, she was the best cook in the world. When we lived with Mother and Harry, there was Cheerios and toast with marjoram. Peanut butter was always the staple, and anything that could be fixed from a box or a can was our dinners. She would bake a cake once in a while but never a pie; she said she'd leave that job up to Mom. Years later, sometimes Mother would fix a roast with vegetables. That was my very favorite. Although in my opinion, no one was a better cook than Mom.

One evening after Barb and I were asleep in bed, Pop told us to hurry and get dressed; we had to make a trip into Eugene. Mom had a heart attack. Fortunately, we were able to get her to the hospital, where she was stabilized and got medicine for angina. The medicine worked for many years.

Barb and I started school there in Dexter. We went to Lowell Grade School. It seems we were never able to finish a year at the same school, as Harry's jobs took him farther away and to many different places. We used the old white trailer they had bought, and the four of us made it our traveling home.

Over the years, we lived in Chemult, Grants Pass, Medford, Sweet Home, Lebanon, Newport, Diamond Lake, Lake View, Portland, and a few others I can't recall. We traveled with Uncle Russ, Aunt Betty, and the cousins. We each had our own little trailers.

We had our dog Blackie, and Guy and Diana had their dog Tippy. For some reason, Barb and I had to give our dog up, but Guy and Diana were able to keep Tippy for many years. When we got back to Dexter, Mom and Pop always had another dog.

We kids played cards when the weather was bad, usually canasta or hearts. When we knew it was going to be a long night with parents gone, we'd play Monopoly. I didn't like losing, but most of the times, I did. Sometimes I'd wonder if I'd ever win, even when I got old. I just couldn't imagine getting older. I thought if I was older, maybe things would be better.

We'd spend the nights together in Uncle Russ's trailer, usually on weekends, when there wouldn't be school the next morning. We doubled up on the twin beds they had. They were lucky; they had an indoor bathroom.

A few years later, Harry bought us a better trailer with a bathroom. I remember the day we got it. We were so proud and excited. It was eight feet wide and thirty-four feet long with two big bay windows, one on each side, and a full-sized window in the front. There was one full bed in the bedroom Barb and I shared with two tiny closets, and one large closet Mother used for their clothes. There was a pretty fold-down couch in the front room that my parents slept on and a fold-down table that could be out of the way when not in use. Just inside the door was a big, black leather chair we all wanted to sit in. To us, it was a palace, and it didn't leak.

I can't recall which one of us kids got chicken pox first, but the parents decided to let us all get it at once and be done with it. So, they kept us all together until we all got it and did our suffering together. When we were all healed up and well, we didn't have to think about it happening again.

Back in Dexter in late spring, Barb and I went with Pop out in the fields and picked up fifty billion rocks. I really didn't count them, but I feel like it was that many because, it never ended during plow seasons, and it was a chore we didn't like. We threw them all in the large wooden wagon pulled by the tractor. While picking up the billion rocks to discard by the barn, Barb and I found many beautiful rocks we collected. Some were white with sparkly purple spikes that glistened in the sun. We found out years later that they were quartz. As we plowed the fields, and I say we, because Barb and I stood, one on each side behind the seat of the tractor, and hung on to the big grey fenders while Pop drove.

One day, after so many prayers about Charlie, Pop, Barb, and I went to find him. There was an old team of white horses there also Pop used to use until he bought the tractor. King and Queeny were their names. Pop put us up on them, Barb on one and me on the other. I grabbed the mane and hugged her neck. She was so big my legs stuck straight out from her sides. She was gentle and seemed to enjoy the attention. Then Charlie came up to us and nuzzled Pop's hand, and he slipped the halter on him. I didn't think he was as pretty as the white horses. He was brown, and where he did have white, it was muddy. He was smaller than the white horses. Then Pop reached up and took Barb off King and reached to take me off Queeny. King was standing next to Queeny, so I grabbed his mane and slid over onto him. I didn't want to get off those wonderful horses. Pop just laughed, but I think he was a little surprised that I did that. We brought Charlie to the barn and left King and Queeny there. Pop rode Charlie for a few days and then said he should be okay for us kids to ride. I was so excited. The saddle was too big for me and the stirrups too long to adjust, but I climbed on him and decided I was a cowboy; I never thought of myself being a cowgirl. I guess I was just impressed with cowboys and thought if you ride a horse, you must be a cowboy. I was obsessed with cowboys and horses and dreamed that one day I'd have my own horse. Aunt Evelyn bought me a leather cowgirl skirt with a matching vest and black hat she sent me for my birthday. I wore it until I grew out of it.

Charlie was a gentle horse, and mostly all we did was just walk him. Just being on him was a great thrill for me. Barb enjoyed him also but not as much as I did. She fed him an apple one day, and he accidentally bit her finger, but he had been gentle about it.

I gave Charlie a haircut one day, after I spent an hour brushing all the caked mud from him, but it didn't turn out the way I had imagined. Mom was more concerned about his whiskers I cut back. She told me those whiskers were there for a good reason and not to cut them again. I wasn't allowed to play with scissors, so I was in trouble for sneaking them out of the house and for the bad haircut. I had a fascination with scissors and gave myself a haircut also. Where I once had bangs now were only short, uneven pieces of hair. Somehow, those scissors had done a bad job on both of us.

That late summer, we went for a picnic by the pond. The weather became very strange. The sky turned grey, and it was very quiet and still. Even the birds were silent. It was exceptionally warm. I'd never felt weather like that; it was surreal, and I found myself enjoying that moment. Mom told us to gather things up quickly and get to the house. Before we got to the house, the wind started blowing napkins and dust, tossing and swirling them around in the air. We got in the house and listened to the wind blow through the cracks around the windowsills. There was no basement in that old homestead, so we all just gathered in the living room. It was a short storm, but it blew down the barn we milked the cows in and the shed where the old Studebaker was parked. The cows and chickens all survived, and we could see Charlie grazing peacefully in the pasture. The main barn where the hay was stored and the cows ate withstood the storm. Then the heavy rains came beating down so hard you could barely hear each other talk. Mom fixed popcorn for dinner on the old kitchen wood stove, like she usually did every Friday night. It was a treat to us, and we watched the tree limbs bend and sway in the wind through the windows. She turned on the Philco radio that stood in the corner of the living room to hear the latest news. We had to listen carefully through the squealing and crackling of the static.

The next day, things looked different to me outside with the milk barn down. Pop pulled the Studebaker out from under the shed with the tractor and propped up the shed corners. The car wasn't hurt much, just one cracked side window in the back where I sat most times we went anywhere. He didn't rebuild the milk barn, and shortly after that sold Romeo and Juliet. He kept the Herford bull and several Herford cows and calves.

One evening about sunset, I was riding Charlie around the barn, and I guess he had enough of me for the day. I remember I was singing, and maybe he didn't like it, anyway, he decided to buck. I went flying off and hit the barn that had blown down. It knocked the breath out of me, and I couldn't get up quickly. When I got my breath back, I yelled "Help, help," and the next thing I knew Pop was carrying me to the house. I noticed he was breathing pretty hard before we got to the house, so I told him I could walk, and he put me down, and I was fine. Unfortunately, they sold Charlie a few weeks later. It was a sad day for me as I watched the people with the truck come in the driveway.

Charlie wasn't dumb; he ran all over the place making it hard for them to catch him. King and Queeny had disappeared, and no one would tell me where they were. I never did hear what happened to them. I cried and cried, but their decision had been made. They kept the saddle and bridle so a horse might still be considered in the future.

Soon after that, I took my red wagon and managed to put an empty fifty-five-gallon barrel drum on it and then added the saddle. I climbed up in the saddle and pretended to be riding a horse. I decided to pull the wagon to the top of the driveway, get in the saddle, and see if I could make it go down the gravel road. I was lucky it didn't work; it could have been disastrous. The only embarrassing part was that one of the kids from school saw me. He and his mother happened to drive by on their way to the store and see me. When school started, he told me all about it.

Once a year, we would load three steers in the back of the green Dodge truck and take them to the auction in Springfield. Pop said the money from them would pay the taxes. I had no idea what taxes were. The auction was always so fun. I would find a pony or horse I wanted, and with excitement, I'd show it to Pop to see his reaction. It was such a letdown when he'd shake his head no. He'd buy us popcorn as we walked around looking at things that interested him. He would never buy us soda because he said it was bad for our teeth. Instead, he'd buy us small cartons of milk. I wasn't interested in farm equipment and got bored walking with Mom looking at quilts, material, and the latest in cooking stoves. At that time, they had a propane gas cooking stove and oven. I wandered off over to where the horses were and tried to pet them through the tall wooden fences.

My cousin, Diana, and I were crazy over horses and would draw them and knew one day we'd have one. Her drawings were much better than mine, so I kept practicing. She let me have a few of hers, and I showed them to some friends and told them I drew them.

I was jealous of Barb because she got to drive the tractor. It seemed to me everyone was better, older, and able to do things I couldn't. One day, I went to the tractor since I already knew how to start it by watching Pop carefully. The key was left in. I started it up, and it started moving down the driveway, that same gravel road I tried to ride my makeshift red wagon horse on. I didn't know what to do, so I started yelling for help. Pop came running from the house and somehow managed to climb aboard and stop the tractor. Good thing it was in low gear. I think I got the switch that time.

Uncle Russ moved their trailer into Pop's trailer park again and we kids were together all summer. We walked up into the woods and found all kinds of interesting things. First, we had to walk over the railroad tracks to get to the thirty acres where it turned into forest. Sometimes the trains were on the tracks waiting to move out. We climbed under the trains to get to the other side. I was a little afraid because the engines were still rumbling. Guy went under first and then encouraged me to follow. Barb and Diana were already on the other side. There was a small pond under the tracks where we found a turtle, we named Myrtle. Guy said she was a snapping turtle. We all believed him; even though we didn't know what a snapping turtle was, it sounded scary. Guy enjoyed making things sound as frightening as possible. Sometimes he'd walk out ahead and warn of the rattlesnakes that were under the fallen trees and bushes. There had been rattlesnakes found in the area, but I didn't think they were under every fallen tree.

We brought Tippy and Tuffy, Mom's new dog, with us. Tuffy startled a bobcat that was in the area and barked and tried to intimidate it. His hair stood up all over him, and he looked twice his size. After a minute or two, he left the cat alone and returned to us. Tippy was smarter and stayed beside us kids like a good guard dog.

We found mason jars and went out in the fields and trapped large yellow and black spiders that hung between the tall, dried blades of grass. Early morning was the best when the dew sparkled on the webs and the spiders were in the middle of the webs enjoying the morning sun. After we collected a few dozen, we put them in a large box and covered it with another box by Guy's trailer. A couple of days later, they managed to climb out, and it was quite a sight to see them all over the side of the trailer. There must have been 200 or more. Aunt Betty was not happy about it.

We went to the nearest pond and pulled out green, jellied gobs of unhatched frogs and put them in buckets and waited for them to hatch.

We never spent much time indoors, even if it was raining. There were just so many interesting things to investigate, and we did not have television at that time.

Sometimes we'd walk over to the barn and play on the stacks of hay. There were always stacks of loose hay to jump in. At that time, Pop didn't have any horses. The neighbors who lived by the trailer park had two horses we would climb up on and ride. One's name was Penny, and she was a colorful paint and liked the attention she got from us. We weren't invited to ride by the owners, but they never chased us off. We used to test the hotwire fence to see who was the bravest to touch it several times. We would take a long piece of grass and touch it. It didn't really hurt, but you could feel a strong pulse run up your arm. It was enough to make us scream and then laugh.

When walking in the fields we pulled the purple clover flowers up and sucked the sweet nectar from the white under parts. That late June, Pop mowed the fields, and Barb sat on the hayrack that was pulled behind the tractor. She flipped the lever when the rack was full of hay and made rows for the neighbor who owned a bailer to bail. The hay always smelled so sweet. I wanted so much to sit on the seat and pull the lever when the rack was full.

Barb and I went bean picking with a lady who lived up Lost Creek Road. She had a son my age named Glen. Sometimes she would pick beans with us, and other times she would drop us off. When it was really hot, she would take us to their house, and we kids would play in the creek behind their house. They had a small raft we climbed on, and we could see through the clear water to see how deep it was. I was afraid of deep water, and I told Glen. He said, "Don't worry, I'll protect you."

One day, when she took us to the bean field and left, Glen and I decided to wander off down the dirt road where we could hear music and see people having a good time. We managed to find a hole in the fence and crawled through. There we saw a table full of food with paper plates on the end. We got plates and filled them with all kinds of goodies. There was no one standing there in charge to say no. Everything was free, so we enjoyed all we could. I went on the pony ride, but Glen didn't want to go. We lost track of time and had eaten all we wanted, so we crawled back through the hole in the fence and returned to the bean field. To our surprise, there was no one there, not Barb or anyone, and no cars around. We didn't know what to do, so we just walked around the field talking about how much trouble we were going to be in.

Finally, Glen's mother drove up. We were wondering what she would say and if we were going to get yelled at or even punished. She asked where we had gone, and that was the end of it. She dropped me off at home and only took Barb to pick beans after that. We found out later that the property we had been on was owned by the Elks Club, and they were celebrating one of their summer picnics.

That Fourth of July, they had fireworks on Dexter Lake. Mom made her famous potato salad and fried chicken. After dark, Barb, my cousins, and I got sparklers to swirl around in the air. We got to sleep outside that night and told spooky stories and tried to count the stars. It was pretty cool by morning. When the sun came up, we crawled out from our sleeping bags and went into the trailer. Everyone was still sleeping, so we decided to go visit Myrtle the turtle. The dogs were with us everywhere we went.

Mom and Pop left the homestead and moved into what they called "the white house," where they had also put some of the cabins, they brought up from the lake area. The house was then the office of the trailer park, and they added more spaces for trailers. We all had been working on that house for several weeks so they could move in. The house overlooked Dexter Lake, with the trailer park in the back. They put up a sign advertising the park. They called it C Bar Trailer Ranch. You could see the sign from Highway 58. It's still there today, with a different name.

Mom loved roses and planted them in front of the kitchen window, where she could enjoy them all the while they were in bloom. Adding a large fish pond and rhododendron bushes in the front yard, made for a real park setting. By the adjoining woodshed, she planted a small garden with rhubarb, chives, cucumbers, tomatoes, and green beans. She made rhubarb pie and sauce. I just liked it plain, straight from the garden.

Most grandmas have a cookie jar kids can sneak cookies from now and again. Mom only had huge pickles she left in jars on the back porch atop a chest of drawers. I ate them just like cookies. She bought a big box of lemons, and I ate them all summer long. She never complained about my indulging in sour things. We rarely had sweets, although she did bake many pies.

Pop bought a new lawn mower, one that had big wheels and moved forward by itself with just a little push. I was so fascinated with it; I asked if I could mow. So, Pop let me mow. When I got to the rose bushes, I lost control, and the mower went right through them, cutting most down. Mom came running out of the house, pulling her apron off, yelling, "Harry, you lazy bastard." I'd never heard her swear before and was so shocked. She looked at me and said, "I'm not blaming you. It wasn't your fault." I think we all treaded lightly for a few days after that.

That winter, Harry Jr. contracted tuberculosis. He was hospitalized in Salem, so we rarely got to visit him. Barb and I could only wave to him from outside. He was in a room a few floors up. Mother was able to visit in his room. He had one lung removed and was in the hospital a long time. I don't recall the amount. Pop had driven us in his Studebaker. After visiting Harry, we had a picnic across from the men's penitentiary where there was a small creek with ducks and geese wandering about. People were feeding them parts of their sandwiches and throwing grapes to them.

Once a month, Mother received a box of food from the Salvation Army that usually had a little doll or some kind of toy in it for me. The toys were never new and looked as though they had been thrown out by former owners. For Christmas that year, Barb and I each got a large doll from Mom. The dolls had matching silk dresses with bonnets. One doll had a pink dress, the other one blue, with white removable shoes and socks. I chose the doll with the blue dress, but it wasn't long, and I had lost the shoes and socks.

Pop rented one of the buildings in the trailer park to a group of people for their church. It was a large, one-room building with a porch about three feet off the ground and two very large windows, one on each side of the entrance. There was loud preaching and singing that came from that one-room church for only twenty-five regular attendees. One small area in the back separated by a curtain was the Sunday school class. Every week, we had to memorize a Bible verse. I enjoyed the memorizing because we got a gold star on a chart with our name when we got it right. In the summer, when the door was open for some fresh air, our dog Tuffy would sneak in. The pastor would just laugh and say, "Let him stay. He must want to hear more about Jesus."

The trailer park had a washhouse with two ringer washer machines and two rinse tubs. There were clotheslines outside or two dryers available inside. It cost fifteen cents to run the washers. Adjoining the washroom were women and men bathrooms. Barb and I put our record player in the women's bathroom, and Patsy, the pastor's daughter, taught us how to do the "Bop."

Her parents were unaware she taught us, as it was against their religion to dance. It was against their religion to do most everything. Several times that summer after church, we'd meet in the bathroom and practice. I think it was fun, and her parents never found out. Barb and I weren't religious, but we enjoyed Sunday school and said nightly prayers. We didn't know what religion was all about; we just enjoyed the dancing. Once, Mother and Harry went to church there, and the pastor, who everyone called Brother Kisik, told them they were living in sin because she had been divorced. He came to our trailer and prayed loud and long one evening. They never went to that church again, and the pastor was not invited back. Barb and I continued Sunday school there.

When we lived with Mother at the time Harry was hospitalized, Barb and I said prayers, and Mother listened. I asked God to bless (and I named everyone I could think of). Finally, Mother told me to just say, "God bless all my relatives." I always ended my prayers with asking God for a horse of my own. If Mother wasn't home at bedtime, Barb and I said prayers out loud to each other.

Uncle Russ took his family to different job sites while he waited for Harry to be released from the hospital. They always liked working and traveling together, so it was exciting when he showed up with our cousins, and we kids always liked to sleep outside when we got together.

Our parents had a friend they called "Scrap Iron," and he came along with Russ to visit and brought Aunt Evelyn with them. Scrap Iron gave us kids a full box of Hershey bars to eat, and I remember I sure did get sick. He said to Mother, "Just let them have the whole box" because she was only going to give us a few.

Scrap Iron made everyone laugh. He joked around and called Russ, "bucket head" or names like "pig face." I had never heard names like that before, and they sounded funny to me. I heard Scrap Iron had proposed to Evelyn, but she declined. It was good to see Aunt Evelyn since we didn't see her much anymore because she lived in Portland, and that was a long trip in those days. Mother didn't drive, and neither did my aunts, so we all depended on the men in the family to take us everywhere.

It seemed nice to have all the relatives around. I noticed that when Harry wasn't there, everyone stayed in the house, and we kids got gifts, and weren't told to go outside or go play somewhere. Uncle Russ was the life of the party, and I noticed how happy Mother was when he was around.

Russ told Barb to go to Mother's closet and pick out one thing that she would like to have. Barb picked out a silky white blouse that was very pretty. Later, when everyone had left, Barb offered to give it back to her, but

Mother said, "No, it's yours."

Left to right: Me, Mom, Barb, Coaly

Look Out Point Dam

Left to right
Tippy, Guy, me, Diana, a friend

Left to right
Parents, Bev, Diana, friend and Guy

*Charlie, at the Homestead
1956*

Old white trailer

Chapter 3
Afghanistan

When Harry was released from the sanitarian, we moved to Portland, where he sought employment as a salesman. We sang songs we had learned in Sunday School all the way there. Harry called Barb "Sunshine" and called me "Shorty" or "Little Lord Fauntleroy," and called Mother "Gertrud." He called me Fauntleroy because I gave some of my clothes to a girl at school, and for Halloween, I trick-or-treated for UNICEF. Once, one of the teachers asked if any of us would donate our milk money for the starving children in another country. A few of us gave her our nickels.

In Portland, Harry learned how to sell encyclopedias. Barb and I went to school there for a few months. I enjoyed that school more than any I had been at before. I just thought my teacher was fantastic. I was voted in as class vice president. That was okay with me because Eugene, the boy voted in as president, rarely missed school, so I wasn't called on often to perform. I thought Eugene was the cutest boy I'd ever seen. All the girls had a crush on him. He was very nice and wasn't conceited about his popularity.

Every Friday night after school, Barb and I'd catch the city bus and go to Aunt Evelyn's house on Foster Road. It was usually dark when we got there. She always had liver and baked potatoes for dinner, knowing it was our favorite meal. We watched Ed Sylvan and played checkers. Sometimes, if it wasn't raining, Barb and I would go play baseball or kick the can in the street with all the neighborhood kids. We did spend several weekends with Aunt Evelyn.

Aunt Evelyn's next-door neighbor, Bernice, who we all called Bunny, had a daughter and two boys all around my age. Linda and I would play "I love Lucy" and quarrel about which one would play Lucy. Once, we quarreled so much we didn't see each other for a couple of days. We decided to play horses instead. She was a beautiful black horse, and I was a beautiful white horse. That took care of the problem.

We got roller skates, and Aunt Evelyn would let us skate in the house, through the kitchen, through her bedroom, the bathroom, and spare bedroom. Round and round we'd go, laughing and chasing each other. She'd always tell us to slow down, and we would for a few minutes. After a few minutes, we forgot and went fast again.

We watched the Mickey Mouse Club, and Evelyn bought us mouse ears to wear. Then we had another quarrel about who was going to play Annette. So, I gave in and let her play Annette, and I played Karen. We got Roy Roger coloring books with the largest box of crayons we could find. Aunt Evelyn's house was a fun place.

Linda had an orange tabby cat named George and a pet rat named Twinkles. Somehow, Twinkles died, and we put him in a shoe box and had a fancy funeral for him in the backyard.

One night that summer, when the weather warmed up, we slept out on her porch and tiptoed over to her neighbor Ted. He had an apple tree, and we always grabbed a few of those juicy green apples when we knew he wasn't home or watching us. He had grumbled at us several times to stay out of that tree. We ate apples and told ghost stories until finally falling asleep.

When her parents weren't around, Linda's two brothers and I got knives out of the kitchen, and walked slowly up the stairs after the ghosts that we insisted were in that house. We sang, "We hate the devil, we hate the devil." We never did find any ghosts, but Linda had a large dark closet, that we were sure some lived in there. If we were really quiet, we could hear noises from all over the house.

Once, Barb was told to watch us and joined us. We all lay on Linda's bed and told ghost stories. We heard someone come in downstairs and turn on the water faucet. All of us were on the bed, so we never did know who turned on the faucet. Spooky things did happen in that house.

Late one exceptionally warm night, Linda and I climbed up Evelyn's big walnut tree in her backyard. We watched the neighbor man taking a bath through his upstairs window. We giggled so much we thought he heard us because his window was open.

Harry had given up the idea of being a salesman and was feeling much better, so we moved to Lebanon, where Russ bought a few acres with a house, and we lived in our trailer on his property. They dug a septic hole that was so large I thought it was big enough for a swimming pool. The school year had just started, and Barb and I went to the Lebanon school. We weren't there long, but we kids enjoyed the sunny days of fall, playing outside as much as possible.

One day when the parents were gone, we went into the house and called a florist to have flowers delivered. I can't remember where we told them to deliver them but we got caught, and I was banned from going into their house anymore unless parents were there. Barb was not involved in that mischief; she had stayed outside while we made the call and listened from the open window.

Barb and Guy had some disagreements and quarrels. Enough so that one day, the parents bought some boxing gloves and told the two to go fight it out. It wasn't a long battle; Guy got a bloody nose, so Barb was called the winner.

There was a huge propane gas tank close to the house we all played on. Diana and I sat on each end of it and pretended we were on horses. One day, Guy and Barb decided to run and jump over it. Guy tripped, but Barb jumped over it. I don't think they had anymore contests after that.

That year, my teacher read us a book in class called *Charlotte's Web*. I put my head down on the desk and quietly cried about poor Charlotte dying. The teacher asked me if I was okay, and I remember telling her I didn't feel well; I was too embarrassed to tell her I was crying over the story. She sent me to the school nurse, and they had me lie down and rest awhile.

We kids slept out one night under the big maple tree in the backyard. That was the first time I'd ever seen a falling star. It was fascinating, but a little scary to think a star could fall and what it could do when it hit earth.

There was a little church we walked to that was close by. Barb and Diana were baptized there one Sunday. On the way home, I was stung on my finger by a bee that had crawled in the flower I had in my hair. I was just wondering what the buzzing sound was, so I put my hand up to the flower to find out.

That day, Guy and I walked home together. I think the girls lingered to talk to the pastor and get a Bible. I saw a marshy stream I hadn't noticed before, and I mentioned we should go down and check it out. Guy told me there would probably be water moccasins in there. I believed him, and it scared me even though I didn't know what a water moccasin was. To me, it looked like a good place to find turtles.

When we got home, we found out Mother and Aunt Betty had met up with the girls and taken them to a movie to celebrate their baptisms. The movie was *The Ten Commandments*. Barb was so sure she was not going to be able to see any movies again after she got baptized, but was finally convinced it was okay. I think she was remembering how Patsy's parents didn't believe in movies, dancing, or much of anything.

The girls had a close relationship and didn't want me around much. I was the youngest, and Guy was the only boy, so he and I ended up doing things together. The girls would ignore me. Sometimes we played cowboys, and they'd tie me to a chair and disappear. I'd eventually get myself loose and find them watching TV. At that time, we had bought televisions.

We then moved to Newport, where Harry worked at the lighthouse. I had never been to the coast before. It was almost dark when we parked the car overlooking the ocean. The waves came so high they splashed the windshield. I panicked. I was afraid we'd end up in the ocean. Mother reassured me that we were safe, but I had visions of drowning. To keep me from further panic, we left the spot and went to the trailer park we had chosen to live. The park was under the Newport Bridge by the bay.

Barbara and I registered in the nearest school that was about two miles away. That day when I entered the class, the teacher introduced me, and I got my seat. It happened to be the day they voted for class president, and I was nominated and chosen. I had no idea what to do but soon learned that in the morning and after recess, I was the one to bring the class to order, by banging a ping pong paddle to the side of the teacher's desk. I also found out that paddle was used for slapping our hands when being disciplined.

My favorite things in school were giving book reports and to be chosen for spelling bees. I was very competitive and was one of the very last to have to sit down because I misspelled. The one I remember everyone couldn't spell, including me, was the word *vacation*. Only one girl spelled it correctly. That was the year I learned how to spell *antidisestablishmentarianism*. That word was brought up on TV and spelled correctly by a young girl, on the show we all liked, called *the $64,000 Question*. We all had a good time practicing the spelling, although, at that time, we didn't know the meaning.

The South Jetty was being built at that time. Uncle Russ visited, and we kids explored the area. Huge boulders, some as big as cars, were being brought in by trucks filling the area. We had fun climbing around on them, not realizing the danger. Searching along the shore, we gathered rocks, some shells, and a few colorful starfish. We watched the boats and ships and fantasized being captain and what it would be like to travel the world.

Guy's birthday was two days before mine in late April. Mother made two cakes. Mother, Harry, sis, my cousins, and the family planned to go to the beach to celebrate. I went to a young couple's trailer a few trailers away to visit before we left. I guess I stayed too long because when I went home to join the family, they were all gone. I went to tell my friends everyone had left, and I was alone. I had told them it was my birthday. She asked me if there was something I'd like to do. I told her I'd like to horseback ride on the beach. She and her husband took me to a riding stable not far away and rented me a horse for an hour. I went on a trail with other riders and was so happy, even though it was terribly windy and cold. The horse's name was Judy. After the ride, I just wanted to pet Judy and enjoy her. I found out later that it cost a dollar fifty for the hour. I told them I would pay them back, but they said no; it was a present to me.

When I got back home, Mother said they went to the beach and had a good time. There was no cake left, and next time, I should stick around and not leave. Also, she said they didn't know where I was.

Before school was out in late May, my friend Roberta and I decided we'd skip the school bus that took us home, and we'd walk home over the bridge. It was all exciting until Roberta's mother drove by and yelled at her to get in the car. Apparently, she noticed Roberta was not on the bus and decided to go get her from school, thinking she had missed the bus. On the other hand, my parents weren't home and didn't know I had walked.

We were moving from Newport because Harry had been offered a job in Lake View, Oregon. The young couple I had befriended gave me a white stuffed dog I had admired so much when I visited them. I had laryngitis that morning and couldn't even say goodbye to anyone. All I could do was hug them while some tears ran down my cheeks.

Barbara always enjoyed school and got above average grades. She graduated from eighth grade that year.

We lived in Lake View most of the summer. Barb and I found more beautiful rocks to gather. We always lost many rocks we collected when we moved. Years later, we found out our parents had tossed them away because living in a thirty-four-foot trailer, there was no room for all the things we had collected.

At the park in Lake View, Kathy and I became friends. She was my age, and we gathered beautiful rocks and decided we'd build a rock garden. We arranged our rocks on boxes and put up a little sign that read, "B and K Rock Garden, 2 cents for children, 5 cents for adults." Naturally, her parents and mine looked at our garden and gave us the money. We were happy and went across the street and spent the money on candy. There was another young girl my age named Terry. Her mother taught us girls how to braid each others hair.

Late that summer, Uncle Russ and my cousins showed up. We kids hiked up the hill behind the park. Diana said she saw a rattlesnake on the road, and Tippy started barking, so we believed her and walked away from the area. It rained most every day there for about an hour and then stopped, so mud puddles were everywhere. We got sticks and stirred them up till they looked like chocolate milk and we could see our reflections.

Uncle Russ was interested in going overseas and landed a construction job in Afghanistan. He managed to get Harry employed there also. They were unable to take family right away but could send for them later. Mother was so happy about the job, she just kept saying, "We're going to be rich; we're going to be rich." I had an old pair of jeans on that I believe was my only pair. There was a big hole in the knee, and Mother grabbed the hole and ripped it all the way off, saying, "We're going to be rich, and you can have a new pair of jeans." I had never seen her act so strange before, and it kind of scared me. She got a pair of scissors and cut my jeans at the knee and made little fringes on them. Then they looked good.

Harry took the trailer back to Dexter and Barb, Mother and I stayed there until he could send for us. Aunt Betty and my cousins left right away by ship, which took about a month at that time to join Russ.

Mother could have gone by ship also at that time, but Barb and I were unable to go because we were stepchildren and had not been legally adopted. The company Harry was going to work for, Morris and Kanooscan (MK), insisted that stepchildren had to be adopted before they could come. We had no idea how long it would take to adopt with all the paperwork involved, lawyers, and waiting time. But the process was started. They asked Barb if she wanted to be adopted and she said yes. They didn't ask me.

Harry left for Afghanistan and met up with Russ. Harry, being a "powder monkey," blew up areas for roads. He also sent us pictures of the construction sites, and some were of him, and some of Russ as they were together. He sent pictures of the people that worshiped Allah and called themselves Muslims. If Muslims were caught stealing, their hands could be cut off. If they committed sin in the eyes of their government, they were beheaded or hung. Harry took actual pictures of some of some such procedures. I saw some. They were black and white, but you could still see the blood in large puddles beside them. As they were being beheaded, they were told by the executioners if they cried out, they wouldn't go to Mecca, which is what they consider heaven.

Then Russ and Harry were transferred to Pakistan to build roads. I believe the paperwork on our adoption papers came through at that time, but Harry would be coming home in a few months, so we did not go overseas. At that time, Guy had been offered money by the locals to buy Diana. It was unusual for that country to see a blond girl. Unknown to his parents, he made a deal. It caused quite a problem, and the deal had to be broken and monies exchanged. Guy didn't realize the extreme danger he had put Diana in and also what a problem it made for his family. He might have even thought it was a joke. It was a very serious mistake in a foreign country; I believe it cost much more to buy her back then what he had been paid.

When they came back to the States, they brought all kinds of presents with them, rings, knickknacks, clothes, scarves, purses, and a couple of swords. They brought cases and cases of beer to celebrate. Then shortly after that, Russ and Harry left for Peru, where they were both foremen and worked construction there with local people. They also learned to speak a little Spanish. I don't know why Barb, Mother, and I didn't go over that time, but we stayed in Dexter. Maybe it was because Mother saw the pictures of how people were treated in other countries and she feared for us if anything should go awry. Barb went to Pleasant Hill High School that year, and I at Lowell Grade School. At that time, I was in fifth grade, ten years old, and Barb a junior in high school, fourteen years old.

One day, Barb had an accident at school. In her science class, she was doing an experiment with acid of some kind, which was in a clear glass tube. She accidentally got it in her mouth and had to go to the hospital. She didn't get any in her throat, but she had a few weeks of recuperating because the acid had damaged her mouth. She also had a bad experience with her tonsils. Pop, Mother, Mom, and I took her to the hospital in Eugene. Doctors were quite concerned as they said it was a bad case. It was scary for me to hear what the adults were talking about.

Pop and I went to the car, and he tried to make small talk. I remember tears flowing, but I pretended that I wasn't crying. I actually thought he didn't see them, but he did. There was a clock on the dash, and I pretended I needed to learn how to tell time, so we turned the clock to different numbers, and I quoted what the time was. Barbara had some bad memories of that day also. When they transported her in the elevator from the operating room, a woman in the elevator said, "Oh my gosh, is she going to live?" as she covered her mouth with her hand.

We had spent several years on and off the farm, back and forth from city to country, town to town. It was kind of nice to go to the same school for two years and not move. In seventh grade, my teacher was Mr. Kitts. He was also one of Barb's teachers when she was in grade school. Mr. Kitts told Mother, when she came to the teacher-parent meeting that he could hardly believe Barb and I were sisters. The difference between us was night and day. He said he was going to quit teaching that year and go into construction, where he could make more money. Mother teased me about it, saying I was the reason he decided to quit teaching.

When Harry was gone, I was happier. Mother was around so much more, and we did more things together. When Harry was around, they were gone several hours a day, so a carload of us "gals" in the trailer park drove to Oakridge, and went roller skating in the large rink they had there. We also went on picnics with friends, and Pop rented me a pony every summer. Barb and I continued to help with haying, feeding the cattle, and odd jobs around the farm. The ladies in the trailer park all got together with us kids, and we drove to Eugene and shopped for clothes. Four of us younger girls got dresses alike, and Barb got one the same color as ours but a different style. We all walked together down the sidewalk to the car, laughing at how we all looked like one big family.

Mother had friends that lived up Lost Creek Road. Tammy would come after us and take us to her house every Friday night, where we all gathered. We sang songs while one of the men played his guitar. I wanted to play the guitar, so he let me hold it and strum a few strings. It was a fun time. We always had hamburgers, and there was no lack of candy and cookies.

Rex, a friend who lived in one of the cabins in the trailer park, had a nephew two years older than me. Alvin was his name, and he went to Pleasant Hill High School, where Barb went. I thought he was so handsome. We were together often as Mother and Rex took us many places. We also went to the bar where she worked. Alvin and I were treated to lunch and given money to play the jukebox.

Alvin gave me his necklace with his name on it, and I wore it proudly. Rex took us to a drive inn, but I can't recall the name of the movie. Barb had me practice how to sit properly with a skirt on while we waited for Rex to drive up. I dreamed of marrying Alvin. I wrote his name on my purse and jeans. That's what all the girls did when they liked a boy. After the movie, he walked me to the door and left. I wanted him to kiss me, but he didn't even hold my hand. The following week, Rex broke his arm and therefore didn't drive for a while, so Alvin and I didn't see each other.

At times, Barb and I went fishing and every day in the summer; we swam in Dexter Lake. I played volleyball in winter at school, went to the basketball games, and joined Girl Scouts. Barb went to games at her school, joined track, and was on the honor roll.

One hot day, our dog Tuffy apparently couldn't find us, so he went to Dexter Lake on his own. He must have been thinking we were there swimming. He was hit by a car on Highway 58. The people somehow found out where Mom and Pop lived, and they all managed to get him to the nearest vet and fix his broken leg. The nearest vet was in Eugene, eighteen miles away. He was in a cast for a while. He never did use that leg normally again; I don't believe he ever went over to the lake by himself either. He had many scrapes and a few life-threatening events happen in his life but lived to be very old. He certainly stood up to his name, "Tuffy."

The last couple of weeks of school, we had a carnival inside the gym at Lowell. They brought in big truckloads of cedar chips to cover the floor. We put up booths and had ring toss, fish pond, baseball throw, and darting balloons. There were lots of fun prizes. Glen asked me to come outside and get some fresh air because it was so warm inside. I had known him for about three years by then. He gave me a ring he had won at the baseball throw and kissed me, my first kiss. I was thrilled. When his younger brother found out, he said he was going to tell Alvin. They lived near each other and knew Alvin and I had been seeing each other. Alvin gave one of his brothers a note for me because his brothers and I rode the same bus to grade school. One boy on the bus grabbed it from me, and by the next day, everyone at school knew what the note said except me. No one would tell me. It seemed to be a big joke for everyone to hide it from me.

Passing notes in school was an everyday occurrence, and the boys just loved to grab them and pass them around. If any of the teachers caught you passing notes, you were kept in from recess and had to write a thousand-word essay on why you shouldn't write notes during class. It was the same if you were caught chewing gum. I wrote several essays for Mr. Kitts that year. He was an excellent teacher and seemed to enjoy all the experiences we kids could get into. There were days we had court cases in class. Whoever had gotten into some kind of mischief, like chewing gum or running in the halls, could choose a lawyer, and we'd have a trial. I was chosen many times as a lawyer. I didn't do very well but was voted as secretary of the class and did well in that. I wrote the minutes and read them to the class the next meeting. Mr. Kitts had us write stories and read them to the class to prepare us for high school, he said.

Late that summer, Glen's mother had an accident with a shotgun somehow and died. No one really knew what happened, but we all knew it wasn't suicide because she had pies cooking in the oven, and would have never done such a thing. People had said she was probably removing it to put elsewhere, not thinking it was loaded, when the accident occurred.

The little church Barb and I attended in the trailer park moved to another town, so we walked to the Baptist church about a mile away. It was a big white church with a steeple and several steps to get inside. The Sunday school class was much larger than we had afore time. I knew a few of the kids from school. Three of us got baptized in the creek behind the church on the same day: Joyce, her brother Jim, and me. I had only played around in the water and had not learned how to swim. When it was my turn to walk out to the preacher to be baptized, I walked right out to him. Mother was surprised. She knew I was timid in water and said I had been so brave. I answered the questions the pastor asked me, and then he dunked me. Several people had come to see the kids baptized, and they all were smiling and clapping when each of us got dunked. One of Mother's friends was wiping tears as I walked back to join them. I wondered why she was crying. I thought it was strange. I had lost my thongs somehow, and we had to walk back to the church on the little gravel road. Pastor saw my dilemma and offered to carry me. I was very embarrassed and shyly said, "No, it's okay." At that, he smiled, picked me up, and carried me back to the church. We who were baptized that day received a Bible that read inside, "Presented to," and our name was inked in, and Pastor Jim Leonard signed his name and dated it 1957.

Russ with some of the locals.

Cousin Guy and Aunt Betty

Wood packing camels
Even the young packed

Harry in Afghanistan 1957

Chapter 4
The Silent Prayer

When Harry returned home from Peru, it seemed so strange to have him around. He was always in a bad mood. The old saying, "swear like a sailor," sure fit him. I don't think he could ever say a full sentence without swearing. Sometimes he'd be happy, then a few minutes later, angry, very angry. I was confused as to how to act around him. I should laugh when he thought I should, and in his opinion, I should never cry. I was scolded for crying. I was very sensitive and, at times, tears would just come down. If I knew I was going to get teary, I'd leave the room and pretend I had to do something. A few of his famous words were, "Children should be seen and not heard"; also, he'd say, "Do as I say and not as I do." And the big one was, if I were to cry, he'd say, "Stop that crying, or I'll give you something to cry about."

He had mentioned he had tried some drugs while overseas. He said everyone smoked different things, and heroin and opium were easy to get and very cheap. He laughed and said some of the drugs made you feel like you could do anything and that you didn't care about anything. He also said they were taken for pain. He didn't mention he was in pain when he took them.

I don't know if Mother was working then or not, but they were always gone. Sometimes I'd hear they drove to Eugene, and other times, they would go to bars closer to home. Once, Mother said the police were involved, but she didn't elaborate how.

Anytime they'd take us to town with them, they always stopped at a bar on the way home. Barb and I waited for them in the car sometimes for hours. There were times it was cold. All we had was our coats for warmth. Many times, we just curled up and slept. Barb got the back seat, and usually I got the floor. I was afraid to lie on the front seat for fear of Harry's temper. There were times I had to go to the bathroom but somehow managed to hold it. It was miserable, but there was nothing we could do about it.

When he got angry sometimes, he would slap us. He slapped hard, and sometimes my face felt numb for a while. Mother never slapped us, and our scolding's from her were few and far between. We would do anything to escape his anger. The only times I saw him laugh was when other adults were around, and they would tell jokes or talk about their shenanigans they had done in their lives. Mother would always say, "Don't talk about those things in front of the kids." She only said that a few times because if Barb and I were around when his friends showed up, we'd go to our cabin. I had a tendency to walk out to the barn and watch the cows eat.

The barn was in the middle of the one-hundred-acre pasture behind the trailer park. It was peaceful there, and the hay smelled so good. Sometimes I'd lie back on the bales and chew on a piece of hay and just dream. Sometimes a train would rumble on the tracks, and I'd reminisce about being back in the old homestead, tucked in a warm bed. Thoughts of riding a horse far away, escaping somewhere, anywhere were always in my head.

One day, we got a visit from a couple of their bar friends. The lady was a barber and gave Harry a haircut. I happened to come in the house, and Mother said maybe I should get a haircut. I thought, well okay. It was a new style for girls to have short hair at that time. I didn't tell her I just wanted a trim or ask any questions. I had no mirror to look in. The lady proceeded to give me a haircut that was so short, Mom and

Pop complained. My hair was longer than shoulder length, and I wore it in a pony tail most the time. When she was finished, there was only about a half-inch of hair left all over. I didn't dare react to it. They were all having such a good visit, laughing, and drinking. Pop said I looked like a boy. I was glad school wouldn't be starting for a while, which would give my hair time to grow some.

There was a new family that moved in a few trailers from us. He had recently lost his wife from a heart attack. He had four children, all girls. They ranged from my age to Barb's age. One was a couple of years older. Tuffy went over to visit them as they were arranging their yard. He brought back to our trailer a pair of men's underwear. Barb and I argued over what to do with the underwear. Which one of us would return it? We decided to return the man's underwear together and apologize. To our surprise, the man and his family laughed and were so friendly that we all then laughed. The girls' names were Sammie, Ruby, Penny, and Delilah. They became very good friends; we kept in contact with them for several years. They were Romanians.

They made outdoor furniture and had a large flatbed truck they delivered them on. I spent many hours helping them and enjoyed it. Gus, the father, had a table saw he cut wood pieces from and made (planks), and the girls and I took knives and peeled off the bark from the poles that made the legs and arms. The seat and the back were of planks cut to fit. After we worked awhile, we younger girls would go off and play. We used to sneak off and smoke cigarettes. They showed me how to get the cigarettes. There was a bar and grill next to the trailer park called the Dexter Lake Bar and Grill. They had a dance floor and served food and drinks. You could hear their music, especially in the summer when they had the doors open. Sammie wrote a note that said, "This is Mrs. Locke. I'm sending my daughter for a pack of Kools because I'm unable to leave the house right now. Thank you, Mrs. Locke." Sammie took the note over to the bar, and the lady took the note and sold her the cigarettes. At that time, they were twenty-five cents a pack. Sometimes we would walk over to Dexter Lake and smoke a few. Our favorites were Kools. People in the trailer park were unable to see us, as there were several trees and Highway 58 between us and the park. It seemed fun to us, and I acquired a taste for Kools.

Also, that summer, the little church that had left came back and had a revival. There were still only the regular twenty-five people who attended, but they were sure trying to reach God with their loud praying. Some were speaking in a language I'd never heard before and waving their hands in the air. They had folding chairs lined up, and we all got on our knees, put our heads on the chairs, and prayed. My prayers were silent, but many were praying through the roof. The pastor would go to every chair, place his hand on our heads, and pray loudly. It lasted ten days, and I went every day for a couple of hours. Little did I know that the Lord would hear my petition. I just hated the situation I was living in. I had been molested by a trusted friend of the family in the trailer park and many attempts thereafter. Although I eventually did tell Mother, she confronted the man's wife but was not believed. I was then bold enough to tell the wife also, and she was angry and didn't believe me either. I told God I wanted to die if he didn't get me out of that situation. I believe I was serious, and I believe God knew it.

Mother, at times, worked at a tavern a few miles away, and Harry sat and drank while she worked. Then after her shift, they stayed, sometimes until closing time. They would argue, and Harry was abusive.

One late night, Mother came running over to our cabin, Barb and I were staying in by their trailer. It was about two hundred feet away with a cedar tree in between. There was not enough room in the trailer for the four of us, as Barb and I were teenagers and needed room for school clothes and study table and privacy.

That night was one that changed our lives. Mother came running over. She was crying hysterically. She had no shoes or coat on and had some blood on her face. We tried to calm her down, but she said she was going to run down to the office and tell Mom and Pop so they could do something with Harry.

After Mother left, Harry showed up at the door. He broke down the door that wasn't even locked and attacked Barb. I stood on the bed in the corner of the room and was totally in shock and couldn't move. Barb kicked him violently until he fell into our clothes rack and couldn't get up. Barb grabbed me and said, "Let's go," and we ran down to Mom and Pop's house.

Pop went to the cabin, where we said Harry had gone, and settled him down somehow. We never did know what he said or did. Mother said she had no idea he would go to the cabin and attack us. Mom kept saying, "He's sick." She'd shake her head and just say over and over, "He's sick." And with anger, she said, "I wish all the beer and cigarette companies would all blow up."

We stayed at their house that night, and Mom fixed Barb and me breakfast. Mother wanted a cigarette to calm her down but didn't have any with her. Mom told Pop to go to the trailer and get her a pack. He was not willing, but Mom encouraged him to go. That surprised me; as much as she hated people smoking, she had mercy on Mother's feelings.

A couple of weeks later, Mother told Barb and I to gather some clothes and put them in grocery bags (we didn't have suitcases). Harry was gone somewhere, and one of Mother's friends came and took us to the Greyhound bus depot in Eugene. We left in such a hurry I don't believe Mom and Pop knew anything. We couldn't take Tuffy, but he spent a lot of time at Mom and Pop's whenever we weren't home, so we knew he would be cared for. We went to Aunt Evelyn's house in Portland, and that week, Mother filed for divorce.

I was so excited to be away from Harry and all the horrible things that happened there. We looked in the paper for jobs. I had just turned thirteen and Barb was now seventeen. Barb and I saw we could catch a bus and go bean picking, which would help us buy school clothes. Although at that time we didn't know what school we'd be going to.

We caught the bus on Foster Road around 6 a.m. It took about an hour to reach Alderman Farms in Dayton. The bus was full of young boys and girls, mostly under eighteen, ready to pick the beans. What a great place to meet kids who lived in the area. After a couple of days of picking, Barb was asked if she wanted to work in the canteen trailer. She was happy to do that. I continued to pick beans. I was very fast, when I wanted to be, and did very well. Our bean boss was Mrs. Slimline. It was a very large bean field, and kids from all over different areas in Oregon came. We kept in separate groups so as not to get lost from our boss or bus.

This is where I found out about taxes, Social Security, and such. When I got my check, I had it all planned out in my head how much I was going to get, and I was excited about my first real check. But when I got it, the pay stub said money was taken out for Social Security and a few other things. I was shocked. "What's this?" I asked. Mother explained to me that it was withholding money for my old age. I couldn't believe it and said, "I just turned thirteen!" "Well, that's just the way it is," she laughed. Talk about a rude awakening. I had picked beans before but never had to pay Social Security or other taxes.

I didn't know it at the time but Aunt Evelyn had cancer. She may have only just found out. One day, we were watching Oral Roberts on TV. When he said, "Put your hand on the TV, and I'll pray for you," Evelyn told Mother to put her hand on the TV. Mother said, "You put your hand on the TV. You need it more than me." I was thinking, *I wonder why they are afraid to put their hand on the TV*. Somehow, I was thinking there was something wrong with doing that. It made me wonder.

One morning, I decided I'd walk to another bus stop, where some friends I had just met caught their bus. It was about 4:30 a.m. As I was briskly walking, a man in a red convertible drove by. There wasn't any other traffic, and I saw him turn around and head back to me. I could see he didn't have a shirt on. It wasn't that warm not to be wearing a shirt. He pulled up beside me and asked where I was going. I told him I was meeting up with friends to go bean picking, and I kept walking. He drove slowly beside me and said, "Jump in. I'm going bean picking too." I said, "No, they are expecting me, and I'd better hurry." Again, he said, "Come on. I'll take you there. Get in!" The way he said, "Get in" was forceful and demanding. I said "No," and took off running across the street and kept running. I saw that he turned around, and I knew he would be coming back looking for me, so I hid in someone's yard until I could see he was far enough away for me to disappear from his sight. I ran through yards, dodging any way I could to stay out of sight from the streets. Finally, I got to my friends' bus stop, and the bus arrived shortly. I didn't tell anyone about that guy. I thought that I would have been punished because I had gone to a different bus stop to meet with friends.

My hair had finally grown out long enough to curl with bobby pins. Even though it was dusty and dirty in the bean fields I wanted to look the best I could. And yes, I was interested in boys.

Grandma Edina came to visit us from South Dakota. We had only seen her once before when she visited us in Dexter when Harry was gone to Afghanistan. She always bought us little presents. I forget what she bought Mother and Barb, but she bought me a billfold with a horse on it. We enjoyed her visit. She didn't speak about Roger at all, and at that time, I wasn't interested in knowing anything about him.

Then Agnes, one of Mother's cousins from South Dakota, came to visit with her husband. They had just gotten married, and she was forty-five years old. She had been a missionary in her church and had spent years involved in reaching people with the gospel. She said she had waited for the perfect man to marry. Agnes's sister, Alice, had come out to visit us also and took Barb and me to the Art Linkletter Show in

Portland. We all took home a trinket from his show; it was a brass key with his name on it.

A few weeks later, Harry showed up at Evelyn's. I wasn't there when he got there; Barb and I had just gotten home from bean picking. When I walked into the house and saw him, I was furious! I walked in the kitchen without saying a word. Mother came in and told me to get out there and say hello. I was so angry and couldn't understand why he was there and how she could even think about taking him back. It had been so peaceful with him gone, no yelling, no drinking, no physical abuse, and Mother was there most of the time.

Mother said they were discussing details of where to live and so on. Then she said, "There's something you kids need to know. He's been diagnosed with multiple sclerosis." We didn't know what that was and had no idea what lay ahead. They had thought maybe he had acquired it from all the dust he had worked around while blowing up areas to build roads. Or, maybe he might have been damaged when some of the dynamite blasted earlier than anticipated, and he had been too close to the explosions. The doctors at that time had no certain answers.

I had met a boy at the bean field who went to Marshal High School, and I had hoped to stay in that area so I could continue to see him. Now Harry came back into our lives and messed up everything, and he was sick with whatever this was. I didn't want him to interrupt our peaceful lives. My life or my feelings didn't seem to matter to anyone. I was too young to do anything about the whole situation. Now Mother was angry at me for trying to tell her how I felt about all of it. And as they say in the big courthouse, you're "overruled." Something happens to people when they feel trapped. And I felt trapped! Angry and trapped! If you don't have any say of what happens in your life, there are only two things to do. Give up (give in) or rebel.

Chapter 5
Rainy Days

We moved to Monta Villa District, about six miles from Evelyn, where we tried to start a new life with all the drama, we had been through as a family. We rented an apartment of a fourplex; the owners lived on the first floor under our apartment. That fall, Barb started school at Girls Poly in Portland for her senior year. It was the only school that offered business classes and bookkeeping that she was interested in. She caught a city bus to get there and did babysitting jobs for several people after school.

    I went to Vestal Grade school my eighth year. I wasn't too interested in school. I got a babysitting job down the street with a lady who owned a beauty salon in the basement of her home. I was allowed to leave class a half-hour earlier when school was out to hold the job. I cared for two young girls while their mother worked. I didn't like babysitting, but it was all I could get at that age. I had other sitting jobs for people Mother knew, and Barb had sat for them also. Mother was working at a tavern, and Harry got a job as a janitor at Massy Ferguson. Because of his health with the MS, he was unable to walk far or upstairs at his job. He began to use a crutch to help him get around. On Saturdays, I went to work with him and went up the stairs and cleaned bathrooms and mopped floors for him. As a janitor, he had the keys to the candy machine, and he opened it up, and I was able to choose two candy bars for my helping him. I was fine with that. I didn't mind working, even cleaning the toilets. I did the chores quickly. I don't know if his boss ever knew or found out I had helped.

My best friend at school was Sue. We had an hour lunch, so Sue and I would go to her house and listen to music, dance, eat, talk about boys, smoke, and then head back to class. Sometimes we'd go to my place. If Mother was home, she'd fix us sandwiches and soup. Many weekends, I'd spend nights with Sue. We would sneak out her bedroom window and meet up with friends. It wasn't easy to sneak out at my place at that time since we lived on the second floor. Sue had an older brother who never told on her because he was into mischievous things himself. Sometimes a few of us would go to the movies, mostly the 104th Street Drive Inn, where the movies let out pretty late, so the police never pulled us over for curfew. We always managed to get someone older to buy us beer and cigarettes while we watched the movie and talked. At that time, you could legally buy cigarettes at sixteen but had to be twenty-one to buy beer in Oregon.

There was a candy store next to the school we visited every school day, mostly just to talk to the people running it, but we bought frequently. The young guy who worked there was about eighteen, just out of high school, and working his first job. He had a cute Volkswagen bug he had named "Puddle Jumper."

At recess sometimes, we would walk around the perimeter of the school and smoke. Once, we stood in front of a house, and an elderly lady who lived there came out and said, "Oh girls, it's not good to smoke. Please don't do that." So, we put the cigarettes out and walked away. We laughed when she was out of sight and mimicked her voice. That was one of the fun things we liked to do, was mimic voices, especially the ones that irritated us.

Since Mother didn't drive, we only had one car, and Mother had to learn how to drive. She never had a reason to learn before. But Harry was getting worse daily, and the doctors said it would not be long before he would have to stop driving. He was still cantankerous, but I was gone to school and working, and when I got home, most of the time, I just ate and then went to my room, avoiding him as much as possible. My teacher, Miss Powell, came over one evening and tried to sell us some encyclopedias. She just came over unexpected. I was so nervous and afraid that Harry would swear or say something awful to her.

There were some programs we watched on TV we all liked. It was comforting to watch *Carol Burnett*, *Disney World*, *The Tim Conway Show*, *All in the Family*, and some other funny videos. It was the only funny things happening in our lives. We did watch the World Series in baseball. We ate popcorn and made it as pleasurable as possible. Those were some of the best times I remember. We all cheered for the Yankees.

Sometimes Aunt Evelyn would call, and I'd always tell her, "When I get older, I'll buy a baby blue convertible and come and pick you up." She had a Ouija board and would use it almost daily. I'd ask her questions, and she'd take that board and move the paddle to letters to answer me. I thought it was pretty neat how she could get it to answer her. Mother said she could really make it talk. We, at that time, had no understanding of what that board represented and didn't know it was something that Christians had been warned not to do. A few times, Evelyn said she went to a fortune-teller. She said the lady told her a few things that were going to happen in her future, but she didn't elaborate what they were. She only mentioned two things. One was to eat dates, and the other was to use only white toilet paper. Apparently, Evelyn had told her she had bowel cancer.

Uncle Russ and family were still living overseas. At that time, they were in Bangkok, Thailand. Russ had bought a bar there. The story was told to me that he overindulged one night there and bought everyone drinks, and the bill came to a few thousand dollars. He was furious when he sobered up and told everyone he'd buy the place first before he'd pay that kind of money for drinks. So that's how he ended up the owner of the bar.

He had come back to the States to renew his Visa. He saw how Harry and I couldn't stand each other and suggested he could take me back with him and stay with his family for a while. But Mother was unwilling to let that happen. I was very disappointed and wanted to go with him.

I turned on the TV to watch *Lassie*, and Harry burst into swearing. Russ laughed and said, "Oh, let her watch it." Harry said, "All those kid programs make it look like the kids are always right and the parents are wrong."

Uncle Russ winked at me and said, "Go ahead and watch it." They went into the dining room and closed the door. Harry and Russ got along so well. If there was one person on earth that could calm Harry down it was Uncle Russ. Just before Russ left, he picked me up and sat me in his lap. I cried as I hugged him. I wanted to go with him. He was about the best man I ever knew.

The boy I liked from the bean bus, Mel, had an older brother who used his sister's car and brought him to the library in my area. Parents never knew what was going on at the library. There were a couple of boys at school who wanted to date me, but I was so embarrassed by Harry that I just met the guys at the library. His horrible temper kept me from inviting anyone over.

One evening, I just decided to leave. I ran away while they were watching TV. I said I needed to do my homework. I used the table in the dining room and closed the door so no one could hear me leave out the back door and down the steps. I didn't know how long it would take me to get to Evelyn's house, but I walked there.

On the way, a car pulled up with two guys and one girl. They asked me if I wanted a ride, and I said no. They dropped the girl off to talk to me, and they drove around the block. I didn't go with them. I went to Evelyn's place. It was late and dark. I tried to wake up Linda next door by throwing little gravel pieces from the driveway at her bedroom window but was unable to wake her. In the meantime, Evelyn woke up, hearing me outside trying to get Linda's attention. She had thought it was one of her brothers. By then, Mother had called the police and Evelyn. Then Evelyn told her I was there at her place. Police came and took me to a juvenile detention home. They put me in a room, and the following day, I received a counselor. She was an old woman and crippled up with arthritis. I figured she was not going to be able to understand me at all. I had so much going on in my heart and no one to share with who could understand. Things I shared with her, and things I didn't dare share.

After a few days in detention, they sent me home unaware of what were the real problems. I never told them the whole truth. They just believed I was uncontrollable and mischievous. The counselor told me how sorry she was for my stepdad, his horrible disease, and tried to make me feel guilty that I was being stubborn and not understanding of his situation. I told her he drank a lot and was mean. I didn't think she would believe me anyway. She told me how horrible it must be for him, and I'd probably be in a bad mood all the time also if I had his disease.

That late spring, Barb and I both graduated on the same day. It was pretty exciting. Mom, Pop, Aunt Evelyn, Harry, and Mother all attended the ceremonies. I had bought a new dress and shoes for the occasion. I felt so grown up in my one-inch squash heels. Barb, of course, got the cap and gown. Mother told me I'd be going home with Mom and Pop for the summer. I was surprised but happy to get away. Mother bought me a purse for the occasion, and Aunt Evelyn bought me a pleated skirt and sweater, which I really liked and wore often.

When we got to Dexter, Pop drove out into the field and, to my surprise, they had bought a nice bay mare. With my babysitting money, I had sent them one hundred dollars to buy a horse, but I didn't know they would actually do it. Also, I knew one hundred dollars wouldn't buy a nice horse. I found out later that Mom had added more money to mine but didn't tell Pop she had. They told me she was my graduation present. Pop said he would start breeding her with registered appaloosas for her to earn her keep. I named her Cindy, short for Cinderella.

While I stayed with them that summer, the Locke family returned to the trailer park to make and sell furniture, which was a good business for them.

The two younger girls, Rita and Ruby and I were inseparable. Gus had remarried, and his new wife had a daughter named Rita. Sammie had decided she was too old to run around with us, so then Rita, Ruby, and I went to the bar to get cigarettes. I wrote the note this time and took it to the bartender. The note said, "This is Mrs. Jade, and I'm sending my daughter to buy a pack of Kools because I'm unable to leave the house right now. Thank you, signed, Mrs. Jade. The bartender sold me the Kools, and Rita, Ruby, and I went over to Dexter Lake, sat under a maple tree, laughed and talked about what we had done, since we saw each other last.

In the winter, the Locke's lived in California. Their lives were so different than mine. They were Catholics and sometimes followed rules I didn't know existed. Penny had married, but there had been a problem with the birthing of her first child, and he passed away. So, they had a Catholic ritual. They needed three young girls to play angels, and Sammie felt she was too old to do the part. So, they asked me to be the third angel. We three girls had to dress all in white, right down to the under panties. I didn't have white underpants, so they loaned me a pair. We did the ritual, then changed our clothes and went back out to continue with what we were doing.

I rode Cindy every day but couldn't get Rita or Ruby interested in riding. Ruby got on with me one time and said she'd never do it again; she was so afraid when I pushed Cindy into a trot.

I went bean picking at a farm not too far away from where many young kids in the area picked, so I'd have some money for school clothes. That bean field didn't require me to fill out a form to pay taxes.

A family in the trailer park who had two very young girls took me with them to the bean farm. I saw a few of the kids I had gone to school with before we left Dexter, the night we left for Portland on the Greyhound bus. We needed partners to pick a row of beans. It was just not easy picking a row by yourself. Sometimes even four of us would pick on the same row. They had a canteen trailer there, and we could buy ice-cream or popsicles. Mom was upset when she found out, she said, "they are taking advantage of those kids, enticing them to spend their money before they get home."

When the adults I was with decided to go to the outhouse, we went at the same time. Kathy, the youngest girl, about four, always called the outhouse, "Yogi Bear's hole." She'd say, "We're going to Yogi Bear's hole. Want to go?" We didn't know how she came up with that saying, but it put a smile on our faces.

Mom would wake me up every morning for breakfast and make sure I was ready for my ride to the bean field. She made what I call "supper breakfasts," usually steak and eggs, or a hamburger patty with eggs. She always had a great lunch for me also. I was never treated so well at home.

By the end of that summer, I had gained fifteen pounds. I was a skinny little runt, so that extra weight was good, and Mom noticed my jeans and shorts were pretty tight, so she made some shorts for me and bought a few pair of jeans. She was still using that old treadle sewing machine but did such a good job that a person couldn't tell anything was homemade.

When they went grocery shopping to Eugene, sometimes Mom would insist I go with them. If I could get out of it I would because she'd insist, I wear a dress. I hated wearing dresses. I just wanted to live in my jeans.

One day in the kitchen, Mom and I were alone; she said she may not be around much longer. I was surprised and said, "Oh, don't say that," but she said, "Well, it's true." She had tears in her eyes, but then dropped the subject. I wondered what she meant but soon was off riding Cindy and visiting with Ruby and Rita and forgot about it.

Unbeknown to me at that time, she had been told by her doctor that week that she had breast cancer. She had never smoked or drank her entire life.

Later, she found my cigarettes upstairs when she went up to vacuum. She was so upset I thought she was going to cry. She said, "I won't tell Harry or Pop because I don't know what they'll do." Unbeknown to her, Harry and Mother already knew, and Pop had caught me smoking before. So many secrets, and yet, people seem to protect one another from the truth.

Mom grounded me for four days from riding Cindy. I asked her if I could go out and pet her. She said, "Yes, but you can't ride." I took Cindy to the barn and just sat on her, out of sight from anyone. The barn seemed to always be a sanctuary for me. That was a long four days not to be able to ride.

About once a week, Mom would invite a lady over, and they'd read the Bible. I knew the lady because her daughter had been in one of my classes at school. I just happened to come in from riding, and they were at the table reading. I had Cindy's bridle in my hands. Mom asked me to sit down and read with them. I really didn't want to, but I had such respect for Mom that I wouldn't disappoint her. Anyway, I wouldn't disappoint her on purpose.

One day, I rode Cindy over to the field where there were several old oak trees. Some people across the fence had an acre or so of turkeys. I'd tease the turkeys by saying, "Gobble, gobble, gobble," and laughed as they answered me back.

Such a strange thing happened to me that day under the oaks. A snake fell out of one of the trees and landed on Cindy right in front of me. I screamed and swat at it, and it fell to the ground. I didn't ride her over there again.

I'd ride her over to the Locke's trailer, and chat with them awhile. I usually rode bareback; it seemed more comfortable to me than the saddle. I always carried a comb in my back pocket to comb Cindy's mane. I'd lean forward on her and wrap my arms around her neck. I loved the way she smelled. She was so gentle and trustworthy. She was about sixteen hands tall, but I had no problem getting on her. I wrapped a handful of her mane in my hand and would swing up. The first time I did that, Pop was so surprised because he didn't think I would be able to do it.

I had always been very active even when moving to the city, and I didn't eat much when I lived with my parents. There wasn't much around to eat. Sometimes I'd go to the store and buy something to fix for dinner for all of us using my babysitting money.

One day, Pop needed to dig a ditch from the washhouse to the septic tank, which was about eight feet away. He said he'd pay me if I wanted to do it. When I was done, he gave me twenty-five cents. Well, that's what a pack of Kools cost, so I saddled up Cindy and rode up Lost Creek Road to the country store about two miles away. When I was almost there, Pop passed me in his Dodge truck, waving with a smile. When I got to the store, the lady wouldn't sell me any cigarettes. She said, "Your grandpop stopped by and said you were coming to buy cigarettes and not to sell them to you." I sat outside the store thinking about what to do when a young guy drove up. I asked him if he'd buy me a pack of Kools and gave him the quarter. He said, "Sure," and bought them for me, and I rode back smiling and smoking.

The summer passed quickly, and it was time to go home. Harry and Mother drove from Portland to get me. As we began to leave, I felt so emotional. I hugged Tuffy the dog and wiped my tears away. Harry saw I was crying and said to Mom, "What's the matter with her now?" Mom just said, "She's going to miss the dog and probably Cindy too." I was torn between staying and going. I knew I had to return to school. I wanted to see Aunt Evelyn and my school friends. So, we left and returned to Portland.

Aunt Evelyn had become so ill with cancer that she was hospitalized. She sold her home to Mother for a dollar, so it was a legal transaction, and told her she would need it for us girls and Harry, since he would soon be unable to drive or maybe unable to walk at all.

We visited her at the hospital daily. She had mentioned several times she wanted to go home for Christmas. We teased her about putting her in a dishpan and sailing her off down the sloping, snowy hill from the hospital, right to her front door.

A few months later, we moved into her house. She was still in the hospital but not able to eat solids, only Jell-O. It was amazing how she hung on so long. They said she only weighed forty pounds. She smiled when she said her doctor carried her when she had to leave the room for anything.

We had to wear masks and gowns to go into her room. She was so weak but managed to say, jokingly, that she was one of the untouchables.

On December 18, we gave her a Christmas card while visiting her. She held the card and said "Pretty." That was the only word she said. Harry had been sitting in the car and decided, at the last minute, to come to her room and see her. He was glad he did.

We had just gotten home from visiting her when the hospital called and said she had passed. I was in total shock. With all the things that were going through my head, tears came. Harry looked at me and motioned for me to come and sit in his lap, and he held me while I cried. The man who had punished me for crying for years had decided now it was okay to cry. I didn't know what to do with all the feelings I was having. And I was uncomfortable.

Evelyn's was the first funeral I'd ever been to. We met some friends at the funeral parlor, and we all sat together. They played a few songs. One was "The Old Rugged Cross." I was just numb and didn't look at her long but saw she was dressed in a pretty pink silk gown. I don't think she had ever worn anything so pretty before. It was a dark cloudy day as we sat in the hearse. I watched the rain slide down the windows as we drove. I hoped no one could see my tears. Harry didn't go with us; he was not walking well with his crutch.

It was a gloomy Christmas that year. We all quietly opened our presents. There was just nothing to say. We tried to comfort ourselves by remembering her saying she wanted to go home for Christmas. Did she mean heaven? We decided to believe that's what she meant.

Graduation Day
Left to right, Mom, Pop, Bev, Barb, Evelyn, Mother

Mother and I on Cindy, 1961

Pop, Dexter Trailer Park, 1958

Chapter 6
The Boyfriend

After Evelyn's death, I didn't want to go to school anymore. Mother was still working at a bar and driving herself by then. Barb had gotten a good job at Bennett and Williams, a tile company, on Foster Road. Harry was not able to work anymore because of the advanced MS. Barb bought a yellow Chevrolet while still living at home and paying some rent to Mother.

I had a crush on an older guy named Harley. I call him older, but it was only by three years. Of course, Harry hated him. He had only met him once. I met him through one of his younger brothers, Mel, who I had actually dated and liked from the bean fields. They lived right across from a grade school near 82nd Street. His family and I would go over and shoot hoops on the school grounds. His dad seemed to accept me as one of the family kids. We all went to a Chinese restaurant, and I wanted to get their dads attention, so I asked one of the kids, "What's his name?" I was told to call him "Dad." So that's what I did.

"Dad" was a beer drinker, and most of the kids drank too. He never told them they couldn't or even suggested they don't. So, because the beer was always there, and no one told us not to, we all drank. He had five boys and one girl. The oldest was Lucille, and another one of the boys was married and lived not far away. Lucille was married but spent a lot of time there at the house with her young teenage daughter. The youngest of Dad's sons was Johnny. He was six and asked me if I'd be his mother because their mother had passed away about the same time

Aunt Evelyn passed. He was such a good little boy. The other boys, Al and Mel, were around my age. Little Johnny asked all the older women who came around if they would be his mother. I don't think anyone really took it seriously.

They had a big basement, and they always had parties going on all summer long. A little music, very dark, and you couldn't really see anyone. I heard Harley had gotten a girl pregnant, and she had miscarried. They had a picture of her and had drawn a mustache on her, and laughed about it. I never met her but did find out later that it was true.

Harley was a big flirt and dated women much older than him. I didn't know this at first. When I first started dating him, he would take me to bars that he was acquainted with. One of the bars said I had to leave. I wasn't old enough, so I had to sit in the car by myself for a few hours until he was done drinking and we could leave. I had been treated like that with my parents, so I didn't think it unusual, but I sure hated it.

That fall, Harley joined the service, and we wrote every day. He was sent to Lackland Air Force Base. He tried to get stationed closer, but was told they didn't want to station guys close to home because of girlfriends. I went to Girls Poly, and Mother was so happy about that. She felt I needed to stay away from boys and maybe I'd do better in an all-girl school. I didn't choose that school for the same reason Barb did. I thought since she liked it so well there I might as well go.

I did choose a business class. Most of my classes were required. I enjoyed the typing class and PE. My PE and home economics classes were enjoyable because I liked the teachers. In the warmer months, we'd play baseball out on the grounds. Some of the girls took tennis.

I enjoyed English but disliked the teacher. I thought he was young and good-looking. He was very conceited and took a disliking to me. I'm not sure why. One day, one of the girls brought him a piece of pie from her home economics class. He took the pie and said, "You're going to have to do better than this to get an A." He was married but flirted with some of the girls and said some remarks that were not proper, in my opinion, for being a teacher.

My best friends were my neighbor Linda and her close friends Terry and Rosemary. We went clothes shopping together, walked the mall on 82nd, and joined up at the bob white theater. It didn't matter what the movie was, we all met up with several friends just to be together. We girls met upstairs in the bathroom, where we all smoked what we had or borrowed cigarettes off someone. Some smoked marijuana. I smoked regular cigarettes. I didn't even want to try anything else. Some of us wore heavy makeup, and I am not even sure why. Maybe it was just fun to put it on, or we thought we looked older.

One night, Linda, Rosemary, and I went to the store, and we didn't buy anything but stole. Linda and I put popsicles down the front of our jeans. Rosemary put a bottle of wine down her jeans, and as we were leaving, the owner said, "Don't ever come in here again."

We three girls went to a nearby alley and drank the bottle of wine. Somehow, some guy friends found us. We were laughing and carrying on. But we all managed to get a little sick. Al, one of Harleys brothers, said, "Let's all go to these friends of mine; we can trust them, and you girls can sober up." So, we went.

After about an hour of being at their house, laughing, and carrying on, Al's trusted friends called the police on us, turning us in. Al felt bad, but it was too late. There was a big window in their bathroom, so we girls decided we all needed to go to the bathroom. But the police knew what we were thinking, so they wouldn't let us go. Linda started crying, calling for her momma. That surprised me. Rosemary said, "I gotta go home. I think I hear my mother calling me."

The police put us three in the patty wagon, and Rosemary and I started singing, "Car 54, where are you" (after the program, *Car 54, Where Are You?*), and Linda continued crying for her momma. They took us to the Multnomah County Jail until they decided what to do with us. After a few hours, they decided to take us to the juvenile home a few miles from there. Because I was fifteen, and Linda and Rosemary were thirteen, they separated us to different floors in the juvenile home. We each got counselors, and the only thing they were interested in was where we got the alcohol and who stole it. We were all separated in different rooms so none of us knew what the other said. I said, "I didn't steal it and don't know who did." I found out later that Linda said the same thing. Neither one of us told who did it. We were released separately, and I was kept a couple of weeks longer.

This was the second time I had been taken to the juvenile home.

I was unhappy and didn't really know why I acted the way I did at times. My friends were going through the same situations at their homes. There was alcohol, physical, and sexual abuse in our families that we told each other but just couldn't tell our counselors. We were young and didn't know what to do, who to go to for help, or how to solve the problems. And we didn't trust adults. We didn't want to go to foster homes because it would separate us from seeing each other and the places we were used to going.

When I was released from the JDH and went back to school, I met Anita at school, and we began to have our lunch breaks together. She was Catholic and carried her rosary. We would leave the school grounds and pray. In good weather, we would sit on the sidewalk and go through the rosary. I didn't understand religions and why they were so different, but we prayed, and I believed that God heard us. She loved to sing, and I thought she was quite good.

From Girls Poly, I caught a bus to 39th Street with my student pass and got a transfer ticket to get on another bus that took me to Foster, where I got off and walked home (which was about a two-block walk). The first bus leaving school had all the boys from Benson on it, and we all became friends. We all liked to sit in the back of the bus and talk. When the weather was warm, we'd put several of the back windows down.

One day, a guy in a red convertible came to the bus stop and asked if we wanted a ride. We all said no, but after several times, day after day of his persistence, I said yes. One of the girls opened the door for me because I was holding all my books, and I got in, and we drove around and talked. We stopped and had a cigarette. Then he drove me close to home, and I walked about a block home. He was very nice and never made a pass at me. He just pulled over somewhere where we talked and had a cigarette, and then I walked home from there. I just happened to tell a girl at school who was in my English class. She told her mother, and her mother called my mother and told her. Mother gave me money for bus fare every week on Mondays. When she found out I had gotten rides from a guy, she asked me for the money back that she had given me for the bus. I gave it back. I didn't take a ride from that guy again. It was easy to say no to him because several of us girls were waiting for the bus, so I wasn't alone. Also, he didn't know exactly where I lived.

Four months later, Harley came home on leave. It was so good to see him. We spent as much time together as possible. We talked about marriage. I was only fifteen but was sure this was the guy I wanted. I got along with his family well and actually felt more secure in his family than I did in mine. When I spent the nights at their place, Harley and I slept together, but we did not have sex. We just talked and fell asleep.

Harley's dad had a boat, and we all went out fishing several times. One of Dads favorite places was Detroit Lake. When it was raining, we played cards. We went on hikes and drove around in Lucille's car. She had a red Fairlane 500 convertible. We'd take a drive to the coast or up to Mount Hood. Once, I drove back from the coast and was pulled over by the police. He said, "I pulled you over because when you saw me, you swerved." The cop was young and good-looking. He asked me for my license, and when I said I didn't have one, he asked me how old I was.

He gave me a five-dollar ticket and said, "You better let your boyfriend drive." That was it, so Harley drove from there.

When Harley returned to the base in Labrador, sometimes he'd get a chance to call me, and we'd talk for as long as we could afford, which was about fifteen dollars for fifteen minutes. I usually took his call from the neighbor's house, Bunny, because I didn't want Harry to hear what we were talking about. Most of the time, Harry spent time at home because he was getting physically worse all the time. He did manage to get a ride to the bar where Mother worked, and sometimes he'd stay till they closed.

It was up to Barb and me to fix our own meals. We fixed for the four of us and would have to call our parents at the bar and tell them dinner was on the table. After doing that several times and them not showing up, we quit fixing meals for four and just fixed meals for ourselves.

Many times, when they came home, they would argue. His yelling and swearing were hard to take for all of us. I hated being around him and wondered why Mother stuck with him. After or during their arguments, sometimes Mother would leave and not come back till the next day. Once, I followed her, and she said for me to go back home. She told me she was going to a friend's house. I went home and went straight to my room without saying a word.

At that time, I pretty much did as I wanted. No one was home most of the time, so no one knew when I got home or if I was home. I was allowed to smoke in front of them and bought cigarettes from them, because I wasn't old enough to buy. My trick of writing notes didn't work in the big city of Portland. There were always adults willing to buy us kid's cigarettes, even beer, if we gave them the money.

Barb smoked and drank very little; maybe on a hot summer day when she got home from work, she'd have a cold beer. Barb's choice of friends was different than mine. She chose friends who were mostly in stable families and had jobs. We were so different in many ways.

She loved school and said she buried herself in homework and jobs to escape what was going on at home. Everyone has their own way of coping.

There were times I caught the bus on the way to school in the morning and stopped off at a restaurant in downtown Portland. I ordered fries and a coke. I skipped first and second class and then got to school for third class. My English teacher, Mr. Speight, complained to the office, and the next thing I knew I was expelled. It surprised me. The office called me down from his class, and he said over the phone to them when they called. "She might as well come down now because she's not doing anything here." I was a good student when I was there, and I felt Mr. Speight had it in for me. He was always rude and said smart remarks to me, like, "Why don't you fix your hair?" Once, he said I was asinine and then said, "Take the first three letters in that word." Some of my friends in that class said he sure did give me a bad time.

We had had an oral argument when Kennedy was elected president, and Mr. Speight was gloating over the outcome. I said the final votes had not all been counted, so "It's not final yet." He was Catholic and publicly showed his anger toward me at that moment; that's when he called me an ass.

I went down to the principal's office, and she just said, "You don't seem to be happy here, so we're expelling you. I've called your parents, and they will be here shortly to pick you up. We've also called your counselor, and you and your parents have a court date with the judge at the juvenile home tomorrow morning," and she left the room. There wasn't much said that evening when we got home, so I laid on my bed wondering what would happen to me. I wrote a quick letter to Harley and told him I didn't know what they would be doing with me or possibly sending me.

Chapter 7
The Sentence

The next morning was cold and crisp when we set out for our appointment at JDH, juvenile detention home. we stopped at a café we frequented for coffee. I reluctantly walked in with them. Thoughts ran through my head (*was this the last time I'd be free? Should I run now while I have the chance?*). My counselor had warned me if I continued to run away or skip school, they may put me in a foster home or send me to a juvenile institution.

Our appointment was at 10:00 a.m. My mind was working overtime just wondering what they would say and do. Since I was expelled, maybe they'd let me go to another school. My eyes wandered over to Mother. She sat beside Harry with his crutch between them. I excused myself to the bathroom. The window was blocked off with a sheet of plywood, and there was not enough room to crawl out of. Just my luck. I said, "Damn it." I didn't know where I'd run to if I did escape, but I knew who to call for help, and that would be one of Harley's brothers.

The juvenile home smelled of disinfectant, and everything was orderly, and I'm sure every child who entered felt helpless, as I did. I'd been in that room before, but it was a different judge this time, a woman judge. I was nervous as I stared at her, guessing her to be fifty or so. She had a hard look on her face.

We all quietly took a seat. The judge introduced herself, and court was in session. She looked at the papers in front of her, which I believe were all about my situation. She said, "I see you've been here in JDH a few times. Your parents can't seem to keep you in school, and you've run away a few times. Now, Girls Poly has expelled you. In this state, when you are expelled from school, another high school will not accept you."

I was sweaty, and my heart was beating so hard I could barely hear her. My mind wandered to the night before about the letter I sent to Harley. What would he do when he got it? Would he try to call because I told him I had to go to court and wasn't sure what they were going to do? I reminisced about the last night we were together and how I cried when his dad, sister, and I watched the plane leave the runway back to Labrador. His sister put her arm around me and said, "He'll be home on leave again before you know it."

Mother sat tearful, as if knowing what the decision would be. I didn't look at Harry to see how he was or was not affected. The judge interrupted my thoughts. She said, "Since you are a ward of the court, it's my duty to suggest that you go to an institution for maybe a couple of years, and counselors will work on your situation. My suggestion will be St. Rose. Meanwhile, you'll make residence here until you leave." I had not realized I was a ward of the court or exactly what it meant. At one point, they had asked me if I wanted to go home, and I had said "No," because that is when I had been taken the second time to juvenile home, and I didn't want to go home as long as Harry was there.

I was in shock about the decision and just felt numb. Words didn't come out of my mouth; everything was just running through my head and spinning. Two years? I thought this wasn't even my fault, and I was the one who had to pay the price. I felt everything was Harry's fault for coming back into our lives and disrupting the peace we had without him. At that moment, I hated Mother also for staying with him.

A matron took my arm, and we walked from the courtroom down a hall. The realistic pain hit me when the matron unlocked the door at the top of the stairs and led me in. The door closed and automatically locked behind us. I gazed at the area I was in: a wide hallway that had rooms with metal doors and numbers on them. At the end of the hallway was a large room where about twenty girls were watching TV. They whispered as the matron and I approached them to give my paperwork to the office.

With no warning, even to myself, I screamed hysterically and found myself banging on the locked door to fight for my freedom. "I want out! I want out!" screaming while pulling on the door. My mind just kept hearing "two years," over and over.

Two matrons took my arms and dragged me to a room where they managed to shove me in and lock the door. I was frantic and frustrated. I believe I continued in that mode for half an hour when I collapsed on the bed and sobbed myself to sleep. The housemother woke me later that evening with a firm hand but pleasant smile. "Are you alright, dear?" she asked. My throat ached and my arms were stiff and sore, but I sat up, pushing my hair aside. I forced a quiet "Yes." "Here is something to eat," she said, and laid a tray on the bed. "You can come out when you're finished and meet the other girls." I hadn't had a thing to eat since the day before, and now that the food was in front of me, my stomach began to grumble. I ate and then slowly walked to the TV room.

One of the girls whispered to me to follow her, and we walked to a hobby room, where there were books, games, and a radio. The girls all gathered around, asking all kinds of questions.

A short, plump girl, named Pam, asked, "What are you in for?"

"Skipping school," I replied.

"Is this your first time?" she pried.

"No," I said.

"What were you in for before?"

"Skipping school and running away," I said, walking away. I didn't want to talk; I really just wanted to be alone. "I guess I'm going to St. Rose," I said, hoping they would stop with the questions.

They all introduced themselves. The one subject they couldn't seem to stop talking about was boys.

"You got a boyfriend?" they asked.

"Yes," I said, still not wanting to talk.

"Got a picture?"

"Yes," I said.

"Go get it. We all show our boyfriends' pictures."

We were allowed to go to our rooms and have a few personal belongings. The only picture I had of him was of him wearing boxer shorts with his foot on a chair and smoking a cigarette. "Wow," they said. Then there were more questions, "How old is he, and what's his name?"

At that point, I walked out of the room and into the TV room and sat for a while. I thought, *what does it matter if I have a boyfriend or not if I'm locked up for two years?*

Everything was planned and on schedule: breakfast, school, lunch, dinner, shower time, and bed time, all in that order. We all showered and were in our rooms by 9:00 p.m. Lights went out at 10:00 p.m. There was no way to be later then that because the light switches were on the outside of our rooms, and the housemothers controlled them. There were no personal electronics allowed, no radios, and so on. At that time, the housemother came room to room and asked for our dirty laundry. It was processed during the night and was brought back early in the morning before we got up. We marked our initials on our belongings.

The room was dark now, and there was no moon. I looked out of my barred window and watched the traffic lights through the high fence. *If I could only be in one of those cars*, I thought. *Or if I could become a bird and fly out of this window*. At that moment, tears fell down my cheeks, and the lights became a blur. This was the most lonesome time of day for all the girls, when everything turned silent and the girls were left alone with thoughts and hopes. No doubt, there were tears shed in every room.

The following morning, the housemother opened our doors, and we sleepy girls yawned our way to the laundry room to get our clothes.

I could not find mine. It was breakfast time, and the girls all lined up.

The housemother said to me, "Go get dressed."

"I can't find my underwear," I explained.

The girls all laughed, and I was embarrassed. I concluded, "I can't get dressed without a bra."

"Well," housemother said, "sit down and eat. I'll find your clothes."

After breakfast, she had found my clothes.

"Where were they?" I asked.

"In the boys' ward," she said.

"How'd they get there?" I asked.

She quickly exclaimed, "The laundry is all taken downstairs at night, and somehow yours got mixed up with the boys. You'd better hurry up and get ready for school."

Freshly ironed long blue shorts and white blouses were the attire all the girls wore. We had our own shoes.

Every time we lined up at the door, we had to count off. This was an exciting time of the day. The boys were already in their class, and the door was always left open. The girls got to walk by and sneak a look in before we entered our classroom. The line stopped, the teacher opened the door, and we girls got a last look at the boys in their room and vice versa.

I noticed a guy from school. His name was Larry. He was actually shocked to see me there, and his mouth dropped as he pointed at me, as if to say, "You, you're here." He was always in trouble with the law and called me square.

School only lasted two and a half hours, and we returned to our home floor.

Miss Shady, my counselor, came to my room to see me. I was relieved, thinking now I could talk to someone who could actually have authority to do something for me.

"Are they really going to send me to St. Rose?" I asked, hoping she would say no.

"I talked to the judge, and she said that St. Rose is the best place for you. I would rather put you in a foster home. Would you like that?" They had told me of a family I could move in with and work for them. They had six children. I would live at their home, take care of their children, cook, clean, and so on for six days out of the week, and go to night school. Then I would have Sundays off. It sounded like a slave job to me.

"No!" I said. "I want to go home. This time, I'll stay in school. I promise."

She continued, "You won't stay in school or stay home. You can't seem to get along with your father, and your mother can't control you."

I said, "My father drinks all the time."

"He's a very sick man," she said. He may be walking now with the help of a crutch, but in a few years, he won't be walking at all. Multiple sclerosis works awfully fast."

I blurted, "Just because he's got problems doesn't mean he can get drunk and come home and slap us around. He hates my boyfriend for no reason. He doesn't like anybody. All he thinks of is himself, and I'm sick and tired of everyone excusing him because he's sick."

She continued, "If you feel that way about him, why do you want to go home?"

"Because," I said, taking a deep breath, trying to hold my emotions back, "I love my mother, and I want to be home with her." (I believe, in my heart, I just wanted to be free.) I also had not confided in anyone the whole truth about the situation. I was unable to trust anyone with the whole truth.

"I'm sorry," Miss Shady said, leaving the room. "The more I talk to you, the more I agree that St. Rose is the best place for you."

"I don't want to go," I yelled. "I'm not going," still yelling. I picked up the chair I was sitting on and hurled it across the hall. "I'm not going!" I shouted.

Miss Shady called the housemother to lock my door and, once again, I lay on the bed and cried angrily.

"Lunchtime," one of the girls called down the hall, and the housemother unlocked my door. I felt gloomy but walked down the hall to the eating area. Only one place remained to sit, the table where Pat sat with her friend who no one liked or wanted to be around. The spaghetti had more sauce then noodles and looked unappetizing.

Pat blurted out, "Who had the miscarriage"?

"Girls," the housemother said. "There will be none of that."

There was coffee cake set by each plate. Pat consumed hers and stuck her fork into mine, took a bite, and grinned at her friend. I felt like throwing the rest in her face but paid no attention to her. After another bite, Pat realized I wasn't going to do anything, so she ate it. I noticed the other girls looking on, waiting to see what I would do, but I continued to ignore her. I was tired and worn out. My anger had taken all my energy, and I was empty of emotions.

Because I had thrown the chair across the hall, my punishment was to wash and clean all the chairs in the dining room, which I did without complaining.

The following day, Pat was released, and the rest of us girls got along well. In a few short days, I knew I would be transferred to St. Rose. I prayed every night that the judge would change her mind and send me home. Miss Shady quit counseling, and I was given a new counselor.

Mother and Barb came to visit me that Sunday. I begged Mother to send a letter to Harley and let him know what was happening and that I still loved him. She refused but said he had called and asked about me.

She said he was home on leave. I was so excited but knew I wouldn't be able to see him. She said she told him I wasn't home and wouldn't be home for a long time. I was disgusted that she wouldn't tell him the truth and felt much betrayed.

She continued, "He's a bad influence, and I don't want you to be around him. There were some letters from him I found, and after reading them, his talking about marriage, and eloping, I don't want you involved with him anymore. You're only fifteen. He's been in the service for a year, and you're just too young for him."

I stopped listening after I heard her admit she had read the letters. I had the letters on my chest of drawers, not thinking of any reason to hide them. I felt so betrayed and had feelings I had not felt about her before.

Several days later, I received a note that I would be having another hearing with the same judge the following morning. I had changed my attitude and didn't have any more outbursts. I cleaned the hobby room, which took several hours. I put books and magazines in order along with mopping and tidying the room. The girls turned the radio on, danced, and talked about boys. I liked the music. It seemed to help my sadness.

The following day, we were in the courtroom again. This time, just Mother and Barb came. Harry waited in the car; I was told because walking tired him out.

I sat in the front row in front of the judge. Mother and Barb sat beside me. Two nuns sat over by the wall, and when I looked at them, they smiled warmly.

"We don't usually accept anyone who's run away into our school," replied one of the sisters. "We feel you will try, so we will accept you," she nodded with a smile.

I looked around the room at the strange faces. There was the court reporter who wrote down everything that was said. I couldn't figure out who those two men were who sat together just a few seats away.

The judge announced that my family could take me to St. Rose.

Well, it is over, I thought. It just didn't seem fair. It wasn't like the court you see on TV, where you have a lawyer speaking on your behalf; no matter what I said, it wouldn't have helped.

I had no one to turn to. I looked Mother in the eyes and quietly said, "I hate you. I hate you." She looked sad and surprised when I said that. Then, we walked outside to the car for the ride to St. Rose, where Harry was waiting.

Chapter 8

St. Rose

It was a long drive to St. Rose, and I nervously sat, wanting to jump out and run at every red light. Still, there would be no special place to run, for I'd been out of contact with friends for quite a while. I just wanted to talk to Harley. He was so close but so far away. If I could just call him or possibly be with him for a few minutes, I hopelessly dreamed. I don't believe I'd tried to escape if I'd been able to talk to him.

The adults involved in my situation didn't realize how deep my feelings were, and if they'd just let me talk to him, the whole situation could have turned out differently.

Every minute took me closer and closer to St. Rose and farther from freedom. With that thought pounding at me, I grabbed the door handle at the next red light, opened the door, and got halfway out when Barb grabbed me. An instant later, Harry turned from the front seat and grabbed my hair. I kicked and screamed with all my might. People in cars and on the sidewalk looked currishly.

I screamed, "They're kidnapping me, help me."

One man ran over to the car and insisted they let me go. Harry told the man where he was taking me and to call the police, as they couldn't hold me much longer.

A sheriff arrived within two minutes, but I had calmed down by then. Mother had gotten out of the car and had come to my side and held my head in her arms, and we both cried. The sheriff then said he would escort us the rest of the way.

"Do you want a cigarette?" Mother asked.

"Yes," I said, but Harry said, "No, they may smell it."

"I'm sorry, honey," Mother said, looking sadly.

As we got out of the car at St. Rose, I apologized to Harry because I knew I had kicked him in the face while I was struggling to get away. Mother and Barb walked me to the door.

The building was surrounded with shrubbery, and one of the girls was sweeping the porch as we entered. She smiled widely and said the office was to our right.

A moment later, a nun walked in. Mother and Barb stood up. I stayed sitting, looking down at my fidgeting hands, and holding a Kleenex.

"Hello dear," the nun said. "I'm Mother Salty. Come with me, and I'll introduce you to some of the girls. Say goodbye to you family; you won't be seeing them for a while."

I quietly said goodbye and followed Mother Salty. I didn't hug Mother or Barb goodbye. I just walked away.

I felt numb, abandoned, and lost.

Mother Salty unlocked a door, and we entered a hall where some of the girls were doing their daily chores. Then the door closed behind us and locked automatically.

A nun, who I later found out to be Mother John, walked up and held out her hands, which were full of candy.

"Will you be my valentine?" she smiled.

It had slipped my mind that it was February 14. I wiped my eyes and reached for the candy.

Mother John pulled her hands away and said, "No, you have to tell me you'll be my valentine first."

I said, "Yes," and she gave me the candy along with a hug.

Mother Salty took my arm and introduced me to Judy Meek. "She will be your big sister. If you have any questions or when you need someone to talk to, she'll always be handy." Then she asked Judy to take me to the dorm.

Judy was a heavy-set girl about eighteen, with short curly brown hair. She didn't have a soothing word in her mouth, especially when she was away from the nuns. She told me as we walked upstairs to the dorm how I was expected to act. Also, that I needed to behave correctly, or I'd get too many demerits and lose my time-out.

"What's a time-out?" I asked.

"When your parents come after you, and you can go home for the day."

"How often is that?" I asked.

"Well, if you don't get too many demerits, it's every three months. You have to be here six months before you're eligible. Anyone who's been here between one and six months is considered a new girl. And another thing, you're not to talk to new girls because if you do, it's usually about running away, and that's not the kind of talk we need around here."

"I just want to go home," I said. "I don't belong here."

Judy grabbed my shoulders and shook me. "Well, you're here, and you've got to behave," she said sharply.

I hate to have someone grab me and shake me, so I slapped her. She then spoke in a quieter tone and asked, "What's the matter?"

I kind of stuttered a moment and said, "I'm afraid."

"Of what?" Judy just shook her head, not understanding.

I continued, "I don't know, just being in an institution, I guess."

I heard footsteps and turned around to see a nun coming up the stairs. She smiled and said, "Go ahead and cry, child; it proves you have a heart."

She then told me to follow her, and she would introduce me to my school sister.

"She will make sure you reach your classes on time and can help you with your schoolwork. Her name is Sandy," she said, pointing to a girl with blond hair.

"Take her to the sewing room," the nun nodded to Sandy, "and have her fitted for an outfit."

All the girls were dressed alike in their grey jumpers and white blouses.

Sandy told me to follow her. She asked, "Who's your big sister?"

"Judy Meek," I said.

"Oh brother," she laughed. "She's the worse one they could have given you. Just let me know if she gets a little rough on you, and I'll take care of her. She's known as 'Little Miss Troublemaker.' She doesn't care whose toes she steps on as long as it makes her look good. What are you here for, if you don't mind my asking?" she said, opening the sewing room door.

"I was expelled from school; that's pretty much it."

"This is Miss Sartice," Sandy motioned toward the older lady folding blouses. She'll fit you with an outfit."

"How much do you weigh, child?" she asked, looking at me.

"Ninety-five pounds," I said.

"Wow, you're a skinny one," she laughed. She took a jumper from a hanger and told me to slip it on. It hung on me like a gunny sack and way past my knees. Miss Sartice laughed again and said, "We'll take it in some."

"And up too," I added.

She told me by the time I was released I'd gain thirty or forty pounds.

The girls didn't get much exercise and tended to gain a lot of weight.

I could see that she was right about the girls being overweight. I assured her I had been slim all my life and wouldn't gain weight. She laughed and said, "That's what they all say."

"While I'm sewing you a jumper, you can fold up these blouses for me." She proceeded to show me exactly how she wanted them folded and looked over at Sandy and said, "You can help her."

While folding the blouses, Sandy asked me several questions, the usual questions that all the girls ask.

"Do you have a boyfriend?"

"Yes," I said, "he's in the service."

She said, "Well, you'll forget him before long."

"No, I won't," I said defensibly.

"Everyone says that; don't take it so personal. When I came here, I said the same thing, but I've forgotten him now."

"How long have you been here?" I asked, looking up from my folding.

"Four years," she said.

"You mean on your time-outs, you never got hold of him?" I asked.

"I've never had a time-out," she continued without looking up.

"But Judy said you get a time-out every three months after you're not a new girl anymore; is that true?" Her answer disturbed me.

"Not for everyone; it depends on how many demerits you get. You're allowed sixty, and if you get more than that, you aren't allowed a time-out."

"What are you here for?" I asked inquisitively.

Sandy looked up from her folding for the first time, paused, and then in a quiet voice, she said, "Murder. That's why I'm not allowed a time-out."

I was shocked and softly repeated, "Murder?"

"It was an accident," she said. "So, I'll be here till I'm twenty-one."

"Come on, girls," Miss Sartice interrupted, "Less talk and more work," as she pushed more blouses on the table.

It was quiet then. My mind was busy processing everything that was said as we completed the folding.

"You're a good worker," Miss Sartice said, handing the finished jumper to me. "Hurry and get dressed. It's lunchtime."

The dining room was large, seating over a hundred girls, five or six to a table. When Mother Salty entered, everyone stood except me. My big sister, Judy, jabbed me with her elbow. "Stand up," she snapped. I really didn't understand why they all had to stand every time a nun walked into the room. Apparently, it was the thing to do, so I slowly stood.

"You may be seated," Mother Salty nodded from her table. Her table was in the middle of the room and stood on a small platform so she could see all the tables and girls.

I looked around at everyone and was surprised to recognize four girls from school. Two of them had been friends. I nodded to them and thought, *Now I know what happened to them*. It had been so mysterious to the kids at school what had suddenly happened to them. I knew the kids would be wondering about me now.

"Eat," Judy glared.

"I'm not hungry," I said loudly.

"Eat something anyway. It's a rule; you have to eat something."

"I'm not hungry," I repeated, glaring back at her.

Several of the girls looked over. A few tables away, Sandy grinned and winked. The look on Judy's face was very angry. I knew she wouldn't do anything or say any more for fear of Mother Salty, wondering why we were arguing.

St. Rose had a laundry room, where the girls worked for an outside service company to pay for movies that were shown on Saturday nights.

School was from 8:00 a.m. till noon when we had lunch. We worked in the laundry room from 1:00 p.m. till 3:00, and then returned to school until 6:30. After dinner, we could study, type, or play in the gym for about thirty minutes.

Every minute of the day was planned so well that there was no time to think of running away. That was for everyone except me. The worse part of the day was, again, nighttime, when we all repeated together the Lord's Prayer and went to bed.

Mother Salty came through the dorms and sprinkled holy water on every bed.

The moon shined through the windows a brilliant orange. My tears made it blur. My mind went back to the last night I had been with Harley and how that moon was so orange and full. It was such a beautiful warm night as we stood on the porch and talked about our future. I don't think I had ever noticed before how big a harvest moon really was. I hugged my pillow, and the next thing I knew I was awoken by the sound of a bell.

It was morning already. All the girls knelt on the floor and said the Lord's Prayer. Although I had learned it when we lived with Mom, I had forgotten it but knelt down and pretended. The door opened, and Mother Salty came in.

"Good morning, girls," she said, smiling. "Today, we will go to the gym and watch the news on TV. We will watch John Glenn in orbit," she said excitingly, "the first American to do so."

There was a half-hour of church before breakfast. I brushed my hair, put on my outfit, and added a little lipstick. Judy said to take off the lipstick, that it wasn't allowed. I looked around and saw that I was the only one with it on, so with no complaints, I wiped it off.

One of the girls that I had known from school was in the same dorm. She walked over to me, smiled, and said, "You'll like it here after a while. God will forgive all your sins, and you'll lead a new life. I'm going to become a nun," she added. "So is Glenda; we've never known what real happiness was till we came here."

I couldn't believe what I heard and just thought that she must have gone nuts.

After breakfast, I sat in history class and watched the huge snowflakes swirling around in the wind. They got larger every minute and filled the sky. Soon, half the class watched in a tranquil state. I thought of the kids at school making snowmen, running and laughing, and enjoying freedom, free to do anything they wanted. *Free* was a word I hadn't pondered on before.

Now that word was all I could think about.

"Class," Sister Little said, folding her hands. I hate to interrupt you, but I think you should read your assignment." We all laughed, and I asked if I could be excused to the restroom.

"Of course," she nodded.

The hall was quiet, and I went straight to the restroom. The window was high, but I climbed from the toilet to the window and tried to squeeze through. I climbed down very disappointed, washed my hands and face, and started to return to class.

I noticed the typing room door was open and no one was in it. A window was open, and I tiptoed across the hall and went over to it. In a flash, I was half out of the window. I couldn't get my shoulder or hips through and became frustrated and angry. This damn window! Two small blocks of wood were nailed on the sides of the window frame so it would only open about three inches and no more. I still pushed and squeezed, praying I could get through.

The bell rang, and I ran back to class, grabbed my books, and met Sandy down the hall and told her about the windows and how impossible it would be to get out.

"Just tell me how to escape from here," I told her.

"We'll talk about it later," she said.

"When?" I whispered. "I feel like I'm going to go crazy if I don't get out of here."

"In the gym after school. Don't do anything till I see you, okay?"

I felt like the time dragged so slowly. After classes, I went to the typing room and decided to type a letter to my dad Roger. I didn't know how to get a hold of him or even know his address. All I knew was the last time I heard where he lived it was in South Dakota. Since he was my real dad, I thought maybe he could get me out of this situation. I wrote a short letter. After I read it, it didn't sound right. How could I ask help from someone who I hadn't even written to before? Even though he was my real father, he was a stranger.

My thoughts were interrupted by the bell. I ran to the gym, but Sandy wasn't there yet. I joined in a game of volleyball to pass the time. Fifteen minutes passed and still no Sandy. Finally, she came running around the corner just in time for the dinner bell to ring.

"I'm sorry I didn't make it on time," Sandy said, puffing. I got a demerit for talking out of turn, and Sister Blue had me clean the room and take some books back to the library."

On the way to the dining room, Sandy said, "There is no way to run away from here, but there is a way out. Do exactly what I say; you'll be here for two years, right?"

I nodded.

"Refuse to eat and go to school. Don't do anything they ask you to. Just refuse! They'll send you to the state institution for girls. The average stay there is six months if you behave yourself," she whispered, waving as we went to our separate assigned tables.

After dinner, we all gathered in the gym to watch John Glenn. We sat on metal folded chairs set up for the special occasion. One large television was set on stage for us all to try to focus in on. It was exciting news. It felt good to see some world news; anything was good that could take my mind off where I was.

The following day, my mind was full of ideas as we all sat down to breakfast. Mother Salty walked in, and everyone stood except me. Judy kicked me from under the table. Mother Salty walked over to our table and asked me if I would please come with her. Then she told the girls to be seated. I followed her to the sewing room, which was next to the dining room.

"Sit down," Mother Salty motioned to a chair.

"I'm sorry this had to happen," she said soothingly, "but your grandmother (Mom) has passed away. She went to the hospital for the operation the day they brought you here, and your parents asked me not to tell you because you had enough to worry about. She had cancer of the breast, and the doctors did all they could but with no avail. I'm sorry dear," she repeated.

I began to cry, and Mother Salty patted my shoulder.

"Can I go to her funeral?" I asked.

Sister Little and Mother John came in and said they heard the news. "We'll pray for her," Mother John said, smiling. Then she added assumingly, "We'll pray for you too."

"You can go to your room now if you'd like," Mother Salty said, as she took my arm and we walked to the door.

I looked up at her, wiping my tears, and asked again if I could go to her funeral.

She spoke sternly this time, saying, "No, I'm sorry."

"Why?" I asked.

"You haven't been here long enough."

"I won't run. I promise I won't, not at my grandmother's funeral." God knew I meant it. As much as I wanted to run away or escape, I wouldn't have done it that way. But all the promises I stated wouldn't change her mind.

Anger came over me more than sadness. How could they refuse to let me go to a funeral of the family? "How about letting me go to the state institution," I blurted out.

Then Mother Salty said, "You know you're your own worst enemy."

I turned and ran to my dorm, flung myself on the bed, and cursed everything. I went to my locker to get Harley's picture to comfort myself. It was not there. My nylons and lipstick were missing also. Someone had taken them, and all I could think of was it had to have been Judy.

I didn't talk to anyone that evening, and when the lights were turned out, Mother Salty sprinkled holy water on all the beds, and I could see her smile in the moonlight. The moon shined a whitish color, and my mind was full of so many things, like how my grandfather (Pop) would be so lonely without Mom.

I felt no one really cared about me, and I was unable to talk to anyone I felt could help me. I was angrier than sad. So much had happened, and I was just trying to make sense of it all.

I wondered what the old gang was doing. I wondered where Harley was and if he was still trying to contact me or if he even knew where I was. I imagined a wedding and how we would live together.

Then it was morning, and we all kneeled by our beds and said the Lord's prayer.

That morning, the snow was heavy on the ground, and the sun glistened a million times through the bare trees that stood so still and glassy. It looked so peaceful, but I knew I had a battle to fight and hard decisions to make.

First, I refused to go to Mass; I wasn't Catholic anyway. Then I refused breakfast. Mother Salty took me to the sewing room, put a chair in the corner, and told me to sit in it, but I didn't have to face the wall. Then she left and locked the door behind her.

I was so used to locks and the sounds of keys rattling with every step the nuns took that it no longer frightened me. I had made my plans, and at the risk of everything, I would carry them out.

I didn't sit in the chair; instead, I paced the room, wondering what my next move would be. *Something has to give*, I thought. I wonder how long it would take before they did something with me.

A key turned in the lock, and Miss Sartice and one of the girls walked in. They busily set to work on some jumpers, and then Miss Sartice looked over at me.

"I hear you want to go to State."

I nodded.

"Remember Janet Westcott?" Miss Sartice said to the girl.

"Will I ever forget," she half-laughed.

"She asked to go to State too," Miss Sartice said, looking at me. "But she ran from there and came back here. She begged Mother Salty to let her stay, but Mother Salty said no. Janet claimed that there were homosexuals there, and the girls would gang up on all newcomers and beat them in the underground tunnels they have. She was very unhappy, but they sent her back. Do you want to go to a place like that?"

I spoke up and insisted, "You don't scare me, and I don't believe you."

Miss Sartice shook her head, "You won't like it there. I'm warning you."

"I don't like it here either. Mother Salty won't let me go to my grandmother's funeral tomorrow; she thinks I'll run."

"Well, wouldn't you?" Miss Sartice grinned.

"Hell no," I raised my voice. "I hate it here, and I'd run if I had the chance, but not at my grandmother's funeral."

Miss Sartice said nothing, and she and the girl walked out, locking the door behind them.

Mother Salty walked in sometime later and brought me lunch. "Here dear," she smiled.

"I'm not hungry," I said, walking away.

"But you didn't have any breakfast; you must be a little hungry."

"No thanks. I'm not," I said with my back to her.

She put the tray on the chair and walked out, again locking the door.

It was late, and I knew school was over. I could hear the laughing and scuffle of the girls. It seemed like forever, but finally, Mother Salty came in. She noticed the still full tray from lunch and asked me why I didn't eat.

"I wasn't hungry," I said.

"Well, now I see why you stay so thin," she said, laughing. "Come with me," and she gently took my arm.

We walked up the stairs, one flight higher than the dorm where I stayed.

"This is where Mother John and Sister Lyon and a few of the girl's sleep. And this is where you can sleep from now on."

"Come here, girls. I want you to meet someone." After introducing me, she told me their names: Candy, Linda, and Connie.

"Hi," they all smiled.

Connie put her arms around me and hugged and kissed my cheek.

"Here," she said, handing me some candy. "Welcome to our room."

I looked around in a daze. The room was like an apartment with a kitchen, nice and clean, and a private bath.

"You're really lucky to be here," Candy said, taking my arm and showing me to a chair.

"We've been here for three years and finally made our way to this room. It's nice, isn't it?"

I sat down and answered, "Yes, yes, it is."

And there on the table was the one thing I wanted to get a hold of: a phone. I couldn't take my eyes off of it. If I could just call Harley and talk for a few minutes. I didn't know if his leave was over, but I felt if I didn't get in touch with him before he left, I'd probably never see him again. As far as I knew, he didn't know where I was, as no one would have told him.

Connie sat down beside me and said, "If you pick up the receiver, you'll hear a ring. That will be the office. There's no way for you to call unless Mother Salty allows it. And take it from me," she smiled, "she won't. What's the matter?" she asked me.

"I just want to go home," I said.

"We all do," she said. "Time goes fast; it won't be long."

It was time for the evening Mass, and I chose to stay in the room. Connie told the other girls to go and said she'd stay with me.

After a short while of conversations about all the things I wanted to go home for, I looked around the room for a way out. There was a window used as a fire escape, and I walked over to it. There were no wooden blocks to hold it from opening.

"I wouldn't do it," Connie shook her head. "An alarm goes off when you open it. The last girl that tried it got so scared when the alarm went off that she let the window come back down on her and broke her leg."

That night, after we were all in bed, the moon shined through the window, leaving squares of light on the floor and part of the beds. I was so tempted to open the window, but I knew the alarm would go off, and I wouldn't have time to get far before someone would have a hold on me.

The only thing I could do was to do what Sandy told me, keep refusing anything and everything until they sent me to State.

It was comfortable there, and I really liked it, but I didn't know for sure if I would be able to stay in that room or if it was a trick, a trick to get me to accept this place and the two years I thought were not fair. I shut everyone out. I didn't trust anyone, so I decided to stick with my plan.

Chapter 9
A Breath of Fresh Air

After the morning bell rang, and we all recited the Lord's Prayer, a series of bells rang. I looked around and saw that Mother John and Sister Lyons were already up and out of the room.

Mother Salty walked in and announced that Sister True had passed away in the night.

"We'll be right into Mass," Connie said quietly.

Connie told me that Sister True had been there as long as she could remember and had been sick in bed for a couple of weeks. "She was around eighty," she added. "All the girls loved her."

Since I'd never met her, I wasn't really affected by her demise. I did think that maybe now they might understand how I felt about the loss of my grandmother.

After refusing to eat or go to school, Mother Salty locked me in the sewing room once again. Today was Mom's funeral, and I couldn't help remembering the days and years with her. How she spent time sewing things for Barb and I and took care of us, for years off and on, sacrificing her time, teaching us the best she could.

A key in the door interrupted my thoughts, and two girls walked in. I didn't pay any attention to them as I proceeded to pace the floor. One of the girls said, "I hear you're supposed to be sitting in that chair," she pointed to the chair in the corner. Her eyes grew large, and I saw anger in her expression. "You better sit in it," she pointed at it again.

Her attitude surprised me, and I heard myself say, "Do you think you're big enough to make me?"

The girls grabbed my arms and pulled me to the chair. I fought, throwing my arms, and striking them. One of the girl's glasses flew across the room, and they decided to leave. A few minutes later, two other girls came in. I was nervous and stood in front of the mirror, combing my hair.

"I hear you're supposed to be sitting in that chair," the colored girl said, glaring at me.

"If you think you're big enough to—" that's all I got out, and both girls knocked me to the floor. The colored girl grabbed my hair and pounded my head on the floor. I felt dizzy and kicked and swung my arms as hard as I could. They swung back at me, giving me quite a beating.

After they wore me out, they dragged me and tied me to the chair. I knocked the chair over and lay on the floor. My body shook, and my hands were hot and sweaty. I laid there exhausted.

The colored girl sat on the floor puffing. Then she looked at the other girl and laughed. "I haven't had a fight like that in a long time," she said, rubbing her hands. "I was just like her when I first came here; I got so many demerits that I lost my first time-out."

At that moment, Sister Dawn walked in. "What's going on here?" She looked puzzled.

The girls untied me, and I stood up, still shaking.

"We were putting her in the chair where she's supposed to be," they said.

"Go to where you should be," Sister Dawn told the girls.

Without a word to me, Sister Dawn left the room behind the girls and locked the door.

My clothes were torn, and I felt like a lot of my hair was missing. I combed my hair, straightened my clothes the best I could, picked up the chair, and sat down. Exhausted and shaky, I wondered how the girls got the keys, and who put them up to it. I wondered if they did this on their own, or if one of the nuns told them to scare me or rough me up a little. I knew for sure I was unable to trust anyone and wondered if I would encounter more beatings.

Shortly after, Mother Salty walked in, smiled, and said, "Follow me." She unlocked the hall door and took me to the office. In the office were two policemen. She introduced them to me as Sergeant Wilson and Officer Miller. She smiled and said, "They will take you back to JDH. Here's your coat. Goodbye, dear," she said, smiling.

I walked between the two policemen out into the cool fresh air. The snow had stopped falling but the ground was deeply covered, and the sun reflected off it brightly. I took a deep breath, sighed relief, and walked away from St. Rose. We walked to their patrol car, and Officer Wilson opened the door. The radio was saying something about a lost child, and Officer Wilson reported that they were on their way to escort a child to JDH.

I didn't want to run anymore. I was tired, hungry, and just wanted some understanding. I talked calmly to them, and they responded respectfully. That was more than I had experienced for a while.

JDH looked better to me this time. I knew Harley's leave must be over, and he was probably sent back to Labrador.

Some of the same girls were still there the day I left for St. Rose. They greeted me with sincere hugs, and I was comforted by them. They asked me all kinds of questions, and I told them what had happened there.

I was in court within ten days with Mother at my side. The judge, the same one who had sent me to St. Rose, said she was sorry it didn't work out for me at St. Rose and that she had no alternative but to send me to Hillcrest, a school for girls in Salem.

"You will remain there until Miss Stride, the superintendent, feels you are ready to go home."

That's all there was to it, a short but final decision.

Mother cried, but I had no tears left to shed. I was prepared for the judge's decision this time and ready to move on to get this over with.

Chapter 10
Hillcrest School for Girls

Mother felt bad this time and feared I'd be gone a long time, maybe longer than two years. I assured her that Sandy had told me that I would probably only be there for six months, that the normal stay there was six months if you stayed out of trouble.

Mother said, "Who is Sandy, and how does she know about your case?"

"Sandy was one of my big sisters at St. Rose, and she just knows a lot about the system," I said.

I received a new counselor, Mrs. Thomas, for the remaining few days I stayed at JDH. She and Sergeant Fuller drove me the seventy-five miles to Salem in a marked state car to the institution, Hillcrest, where I'd reside for, in the judge's words, "until Miss Stride feels you are ready to go home."

On the way there, Mrs. Thomas offered me a cigarette, which I greatly accepted and smoked along with her. It had been weeks since I'd had a smoke, and they made me dizzy, and my nervous body became relaxed and talkative.

"What's it like at Hillcrest?" I asked.

"Oh, I really don't know," she answered.

"Do they let you go bean picking and stuff to earn money?" I asked.

"Yes, I'm sure they do," she answered.

"Can the girls go horseback riding or anything like that?" I continued.

"I believe they have some kind of program where you go different places and do things," she added, lighting up another cigarette.

I thought it was strange they were taking me to a place they didn't seem to know much about.

Upon our arrival, I looked at the old brick buildings surrounding the nice green lawn with swings and tetherballs. There was no fence. The closest building around was Fairview, a facility for people with developmental disabilities. It was in the country surrounded by acres of fir trees. A few miles away was the men's state penitentiary.

It was all so different. I had been around the area only once before when my family had gone to the hospital, where Harry had been, and later that day had gone on a picnic. I remembered how Mother had said, "There's the penitentiary" and how Barbara and I had wondered what kind of people were there, knowing that they were there for doing bad things, like murder. I never guessed that one day, I'd be in one of those facilities looking out and for the simple reason for skipping school and running away.

We walked inside, entering the office. It was small and full of bookshelves, reaching almost to the ceiling. The superintendent, Miss Stride, was a tall middle-aged woman who spoke kindly but with authority.

"You will have a counselor in a couple of days. You can write your parents once a day for two weeks, but after that, it is once a week," she stated. Then she added, "If you behave yourself and do well, you will most likely be able to go home in six months."

I was delighted to hear those words and got the nerve to ask her if I could write my boyfriend. She plainly stated I'd have to discuss that with my counselor. "If she feels it's necessary for your adjustment and good behavior here, she will probably consent to it." Then, she added, "Your parents will have to agree."

Then she took me upstairs to a large room with the so-familiar scene of locked doors and barred windows.

"Here is a newcomer," Miss Stride said, putting her arm on my shoulder as she introduced me to the housemother, Mrs. Eller. She nodded at the other woman sitting at the desk, saying her name was Mrs. Cloth.

"This is called Admittance Cottage, Mrs. Cloth smiled. Have you had your examinations yet?"

Miss Stride spoke for me, "No, she just arrived here; she'll have to be quarantined till tomorrow."

I was taken to a bathroom and given some ointment to put on my pubic hairs and armpits. She said if I refused, she would have to do it, so I did it. I asked her what the stuff was, and she said it kills lice and other such stuff.

Then I was taken to a room where I would spend the night before my examination. Several girls stared at me from the lobby. I was given a radio and a warm smile as I was locked in the room. It was a large room with two beds. I stood at the window, watching the few cars that passed.

Well, I'm here, I thought. *I'm out of St. Rose, and this place can't be any worse. Six months won't be too long, I'll probably be out by the time Harley comes home on his next leave.*

I lay on the bed staring at the ceiling, listening to records; the girls in the lobby were playing on the phonograph. They were laughing, and I wished I could be out there with them; I was feeling so lonely.

When the girls were taken to the dining room for dinner, a tray was brought to me. I was hungry and grateful and ate everything. I turned on the radio, and my favorite song was playing. The song was, "Runaway," by Roy Orbison. I danced alone to the tune, pretending I had a partner.

The night was cool, but I slept well, better than I had for a long while. I didn't wake up till I heard a buzzer. I was brought a breakfast tray, and Mrs. Cloth said that in a couple of hours, another new girl would be joining me.

About an hour later, Mrs. Cloth unlocked my door and, to my surprise, a girl I knew when I had gone to grade school in Lowell was brought in.

"Donna," I said, and I was thrilled. We hugged each other, and Mrs. Cloth said, "You two know each other, huh? Well, you'll have a lot to talk over. You'll have your examinations today after lunch," she said, closing the door.

"Oh Donna," I said. "I can't believe it. I'm so glad I'm not alone. I've been so lonesome."

"What did you do to get here?" Donna asked, still holding my hands and smiling.

"I was expelled from school, and the judge sent me to St. Rose for two years. Then I found out if I could get out of there and come here, I'd probably only have to spend six months locked up. So, I did what I had to do to get out of there."

"What are you doing here?" I asked inquisitively.

"Well," Donna began. "I went to a party and got smashed. I don't remember everything, but my friend Joyce told me about it later. The neighbors called the cops, and half of us ended up in jail. When they called my mom to come after me, she said no; I got myself into it, and I can get myself out of it. So, to make a long story short, the judge sent me here. It'd been worth it if I could remember the party," she laughed. "Joyce got to go home, the lucky devil. She's got her own apartment. She's probably at a party right now. That's all we've been doing lately. I quit school, ya know."

"How'd you manage that?" I asked, walking over to the window. She seemed so different than I remembered her.

"I just quit," Donna said, bouncing on the bed.

"What about your mom and dad?" I said. "Didn't they say anything?"

"My dad died a couple of years ago. As a matter of fact, that's when I quit, I guess. I sort of moved in with Joyce this last summer and never left. We had a ball together; she knows some groovy guys from college."

After lunch, Mrs. Eller took us downstairs to the doctor's office. Donna went in first, and I waited on a bench in the hall. Two girls from one of the other buildings walked through the hall door. I smiled, and they smiled back.

"Are you waiting to see the doctor?" one of the girls asked.

"Yes," I said quietly. I was nervous and getting impatient. This will be my first pelvic," I said, feeling flushed.

Both girls laughed, and one said, "There's nothing to it. Hey, you're white as a sheet; you really are scared, aren't you?"

I just nodded.

"Do you think you're pregnant" the other girl whispered.

I couldn't help but laugh. "I'm a virgin," I said slowly.

"A virgin," they said, looking shocked. "What the hell are you here for?"

At that moment, the doctor called me in. Donna came out and said she'd wait for me and sat down by the other two girls.

I walked in, and the nurse was sterilizing some instruments. The doctor told me to strip from the waist down and sit on the examining table. I looked at the nurse nervously and asked, "Why do I have to have a pelvic?" I paused, then said, "I'm not pregnant." The nurse laughed and said, "It's not just a pregnancy test; it's to check for venereal diseases also." I could hear the girls laughing in the hall, and I felt embarrassed.

After the examination, I walked out into the hall, and the girls all grinned. I felt dizzy and warm and was expressionless. We went up the stairs and back to our room until the results on our tests were known.

"How long will it be?" I asked Mrs. Cloth.

"Oh, they'll know by tomorrow morning."

"I still don't know why I had to have the pelvic," I insisted. "My mom wouldn't have allowed it if she'd known."

"Your mother has no say about you anymore," Mrs. Cloth spoke sternly. "You're a ward of the court."

The time went fast, and two days later, after I made friends with other girls, Donna and I decided to keep our room together. We even got the same counselor, a petite young lady about twenty-three years old. Her name was Mrs. Snider.

After staying in Admittance Cottage for two weeks, we were able to start school. We were not allowed out of the buildings, so we transferred to school through the underground tunnels and also through the tunnels to go to the dining room, in the next building. I had heard that the girls would beat you if they found you in the tunnel alone. Many rumors went around of how the girls became homosexuals after they were transferred from Admittance Cottage to another building. The girls called them "fruits."

There was church every Sunday, but I chose to stay in my room. I hadn't been to church since grade school and wasn't sure if God existed any more. If he did, I felt like he wasn't listening to me now.

The preacher, Mr. Fold, came every Saturday afternoon, and all the girls sat in a circle with him and had group therapy. Most of the girls talked readily, keeping the conversation going. Many of the girls spoke of their boyfriends and how they had loved them and missed them. They sometimes cried together. I never joined in their conversations. I didn't want the group to know about my personal feelings or the problems I had at home.

After two Saturday sessions, Mrs. Cloth noticed I had not participated in any group therapy even though I had adjusted quite well to the surroundings, all the girls liked me, and I kept busy with arts and crafts. Mrs. Cloth felt I needed someone to talk to. So that Friday, she made an appointment for me with the school's psychiatrist.

I was surprised when she told me she had made an appointment. I asked why I had to see a psychiatrist.

"It's for your own good," she said. "I noticed that you made no attempt to talk when Reverend Fold comes on Saturdays."

"I don't want all my problems discussed among everybody," I said defensively.

"You have to talk to someone," she answered sympathetically.

"I do talk. I talk to Donna everyday about the problems I had at home."

"Well dear, that's good, but you need to talk to someone who is able to help you. It's nice you've put your trust in Donna, but she can't help you. You see, if she could, she wouldn't be here. Do you understand?"

I just nodded and walked into the lobby, joining the other girls. Not quite feeling myself, I motioned Donna over and told her about it.

"I've been to a dozen psychiatrists," Donna said, picking up a deck of cards. They just ask you a bunch of dumb questions and that's it. Now, how about some poker?"

I nodded.

That Friday, I saw Mrs. Snider and asked if I could write to Harley.

She said she saw no harm in it since he was so far away but she added that I'd have to get permission from your parents.

"By the way," she added, "they'll be here Tuesday. I got a letter from your mother today. Why don't we ask them then?" she decided.

"Will you be there with me when I ask," I questioned hopefully.

"I don't think that will be necessary; you'll want to spend all the time you can with them, I'll talk to them afterward for a few minutes. I'm pleased with your records so far. The housemothers have written nothing but good reports on you. Keep up the good work. It will make a difference as far as how long you stay here," and she added with a grin, "it may even decide whether you write Harley or not. Speaking of Harley, he found out where you are somehow because here's a letter from him to you. You understand I had to open it and read it, don't you?"

I nodded and very shakily reached for the letter and opened it.

I was so overwhelmed with joy to know he still cared. I wished I could write back to let him know how I felt, but Mrs. Snider assured me she would write instead and let him know how I was doing and how happy I was to hear from him.

I told her, "I don't think you know how much I want to write him."

She smiled and winked and said, "Yes, I think I can."

I wanted to hold that letter and keep it with me and read over and over, but they would not let me keep it.

She then told me to go down the hall to Dr. Willow's room number 12. "She wants to ask you a few questions." I slowly walked down the hall.

I could see her silhouette from the frosted glass door and sign that said, "Dr. Willow, Psychiatrist." I slowly turned the doorknob and walked in.

"Dr. Willows," I asked, still holding the doorknob.

"Yes," she said, taking her glasses off and rubbing her nose. "Come in; I'm expecting you. Have a seat," she motioned to a nice comfortable chair.

I sat nervously, fidgeting with my hair, and crossing and uncrossing my legs.

"Relax," she said, putting down what looked like pieces of a puzzle in front of me. "This is a puzzle of a car; I want you to put it together."

I began putting the pieces together. I managed to get all but the last few pieces. No matter which way I put them, they wouldn't fit. I became frustrated, and my eyes began to tear.

"That's fine," she said, scooping up the uncompleted puzzle. "Now I want you to repeat after me these following groups of numbers: 650, 224."

I repeated, "650, 224."

"7984, 6921," she said.

I repeated, still holding back tears, "7984, 6921."

"That's fine. Now tell me what you would do if you were in the woods alone, and a bear came after you."

The question surprised me, but I said I'd shoot it, and tried to smile.

"Good," she said. After a short pause, she said, "I've read your records; your father has MS, does he not?"

I nodded.

"Why can't you seem to get along with him?" she questioned.

"He doesn't work, and he drinks all the time. Mother works at a tavern, and he spends all his time there, and when they come home, they fight. She gets angry and leaves. I've followed her, and when I catch up with her, she tells me to go back home, that she'll come home later. She would hug me and tell me she loves me, and she knew I loved her cause I went after her." I then could not hold the tears back.

Dr. Willows looked puzzled. "Your father isn't walking too well, is he?"

I shook my head and wiped my eyes.

"I don't imagine your father can get a job in his condition; insurance companies won't insure a man with an incurable disease."

"That's no excuse for him to yell and sometimes slap us."

"Tell me, how would you feel if you were healthy for years, then became crippled? How would you act, and how would you feel? Can you imagine what a person would go through in his mind, knowing that someday shortly, he wouldn't be able to walk at all, and in a few years, he'd die. Your parents may both be immature, but there are places where they can seek help. In the meantime, while they are trying to solve their problems, you are better off to be here. Do you have anyone else in the family you could live with?"

"Barbara, my sister, has an apartment. Can I live with her?"

"Is she twenty-one?"

"No, but she's graduated and has a good job."

"A guardian must be twenty-one. Is there anyone else?"

"Well, my grandfather. My grandmother died about a month ago, and he's all alone. He could use my help around the place. He's got a trailer park and some cows and horses."

"Is there another woman living there now?"

"No, just him."

Dr. Willows shook her head. "There has to be a woman there. The court wouldn't allow you to live there without a woman around."

"Why not?" I asked.

"For any girl who goes to a different home other than her own, there has to be a woman guardian. Those are the rules. Is there anyone else?"

"No," I said.

"Would you like to go to a foster home?"

"No," I said abruptly.

"Why," she questioned.

"I just don't want to."

Dr. Willows could tell I was very upset, so she finalized the conversation and said, "You must love your parents very much to want to go back."

On the way back to my room, I pondered the questions she had asked me and talked to Donna when I got back.

"You want to know why I don't want to go to a foster home and just want to go back home?"

Donna stood motionless, waiting for my answer.

"I want to go home because I miss my friends. They all live around the area I live, and besides, I can get a hold of Harley's address from his brother. That's not the only reason. I miss my mom, I really do. As far as my stepdad's concerned, he can go to hell." Pausing a moment, I said, "I kind of miss my sister too, even though she wouldn't mail a letter for me."

"I know what you mean," Donna said, sitting on the bed and brushing her hair. "My mom would let me rot in jail, but I still want to go home.

Mrs. Snider has tried to get me to go to a foster home and start school again, but I won't. I'm so far behind in school now that it just wouldn't work. I guess they're going to put me to work here in the kitchen every day. That's better than going to school, though," she laughed.

"Mrs. Snider is nice, isn't she?" I said.

"Yeah. I like her," Donna smiled, still brushing her hair. After a short pause, she said, "What are you going to do your first day out?"

"What do you mean, my first day out or when I get out for good?"

"Both," Donna laughed.

"I'd like to buy a pack of cigarettes and a six-pack. Just sit back and relax and see Harley. What will you do?"

"Same thing, only with my boyfriend, not yours." Then we both laughed.

It seemed nice to have a friend to talk to and reminisce about what our plans would be when we got out. We had so much to talk about, including our time at Lowell Grade School. We wondered what some of the other kids might be doing that were in our classes.

I took out my needlework I had started to give my hands something to do. When it would be finished, it would read US Air Force.

In school, the only class I had where we were able to talk was art class. The teacher, Mrs. Dee, was tall and thin and wore little granny glasses. One of the girls in the class asked me if I was a fruit, and I said no. I only talked when someone talked to me. I found that there were only a few girls who were homosexual, so I tried to avoid them.

I found the teachers to be likable, and after school was over, upon returning back through the tunnel to Admittance Cottage, I told Donna all about it. Donna had a lot of news too. Mrs. Snider took her over to the kitchen where she would work for the remaining time she was there.

The ice was broken for the girls who were shortly to leave Admittance Cottage to be transferred to another building. There were very few new girls admitted because the space was limited. The girls were transferred and housed by age and attitude groups.

The largest building, building number two, had four sections, Sigma, Kappa, Gamma, and Theta, the building where the dining room was. Each section had fifteen to twenty girls. The building, made of brick, was the newest building on the campus and even smelled new. The girls in this building hoped to be transferred to the Freedom building, Scott One or Scott Two. Scott building had two floors, Scott one was on the bottom floor, Scott two was on the second floor. From there, they were able to go outside on the campus, (also called the Green) every day, and on Sundays, able to leave the campus with their parents. Everyone had to be back on campus by 7 p.m.

Some of the girls were directly transferred from Admittance Cottage to the Scott building for extremely good behavior.

A section of the Admittance Cottage building, above Miss Strides office was called Patterson. This is where the hard-to-manage girls went, and they had housefathers.

There was the small brick building behind Scott that was called "Treatment ward" for when the girls did something wrong, like running away or fighting. It was called TW for short. It had cement floors and barred doors. The girls were allowed a radio and a blanket and a visit from the reverend once a day while they were there. If you were in Scott One or Scott Two building and were sent to TW, you were unable to return to the Freedom building, you were sent back to the original floor you had been on.

The time had gone fast, and that day, my parents were going to visit. To my surprise, a note was sent to my classroom, and I was excused. The note read: "Mrs. Snider's office." I went through the tunnel and up to the huge, locked doors at the end. Another girl was there, banging and kicking on the doors.

"You have to do this," she said angrily, to get their attention. "If you didn't, you'd stand here all damn day. They can't hear you in their offices unless you make a lot of noise."

I was somewhat puzzled, but after one of the counselors opened the doors and I saw my mother and sister, all my thoughts disappeared for the moment. I hadn't noticed Mrs. Snider standing there; I went right to Mother and hugged her delightfully.

"I'm glad to see you," I blurted out. Mrs. Snider excused herself and showed us to a conference room, saying she'd talk to both of us later.

Mother said, "Your dad says hi. He's sorry he couldn't make it; his legs ache all the time, and he has a hard time walking."

I made a quick reply, "Don't call him my dad; he's not my real dad."

"Yes, he is, honey," she calmly replied. "He legally adopted you and Barbara several years ago. Let me tell you something I never told you before." She continued.

"He worked construction and had to leave town for a couple of days once in a while. Well, this one time when he left, you became very sick. You became so sick I had to take you to the hospital. The doctor said you were having convulsions, and I'd better get hold of my husband. So, I did, and when your father walked into the hospital room, you stood up in your crib, reached out your arms, and said, 'Daddy!'

"Then the doctor explained what was wrong. He said you missed him so much that he needed to start paying less attention to you, so when he left on business, you could normally live without him. So, he did what he was told to do.

"I don't know what was worse, too much attention or not enough. A person doesn't know where to draw the line. It's really no one's fault you two don't get along. Just let it go."

"Ok," I grumbled. I didn't really believe her story. It didn't sound like it could be possible. I thought there probably had been something physically wrong with me, and no one checked it out thoroughly.

"What about Harley? Are you going to let me write him?"

"I'll talk to your dad about it, and the next time I see you, I'll give you an answer."

"When will that be," I asked, pleading.

"In a couple of weeks, honey. Please don't be so pushy. Your father wanted me to tell you he loves you and misses you very much. Your counselor says you're doing really well. Keep it up," her voice lightened. "You'll be home before you know it."

"I'll be transferred in a couple of days to one of the other cottages. I hope Scott Cottage. One of the other girls in my cottage was transferred to Scott right away. I saw her Sunday leaving with her parents for the day. I sure envied her."

"Well, it shouldn't be long, dear, till you're leaving too. We've got to go now, honey. Maybe we'll see you next week on Tuesday. Maybe your dad will feel better and come along."

Mrs. Snider wrote an absentee note for me, and after hugging Mother and Barb goodbye, I returned to school through the tunnel. I pounded and kicked on the door as I had observed earlier, and the principal came from her office and unlocked the doors.

A few short days later, I had become accustomed to school and the girls and found that most of the rumors I had heard were untrue.

That evening after dinner, Mrs. Cloth handed me a pink slip.

"What's this," I asked, studying the paper.

"An LP," Mrs. Cloth answered, with raised eyebrows.

"What's an LP?" I asked.

"A lost privilege. We received a note from your art teacher that you were heard swearing. Now you will have to go to your room for the rest of the evening."

Donna overheard as she stood by the office door and laughed. "Guess what, everybody," Donna said loudly, walking into the lobby where all the girls were sitting. "She got an LP for swearing."

"What did you say?" Donna looked at me smiling.

"I think I said damn. I'm not quite sure," I said.

"All she said was damn," Donna repeated, still laughing.

Mrs. Cloth took Donna by the arm and motioned to me to follow. "Now you both have LPs," she said and locked the door behind us.

We could hear the girls in the lobby still laughing, and Mrs. Cloth told them to settle down or they'd all have LPs.

Since Donna and I shared the same room, we turned on the radio and talked about our boyfriends and utterly enjoyed our LPs.

The following day, Mrs. Snider told me I would be transferred to the cottage floor Theta.

"How come?" I asked, still hoping I had a chance for Scott.

"You got an LP last night, didn't you?" she asked.

"Yes, but," I paused, "you mean that's the only reason that stopped me?"

"No," Mrs. Snider said, handing me a slip of paper. It's mostly your attitude. You're not taking things as serious as you should. Stay out of trouble now, and you can be transferred to Scott in a short time. Don't miss school, keep your room clean, and get along with the girls. I'll see you later, go on over through the tunnel; there is someone to meet you there and take you to your floor."

Hillcrest
Salem Oregon

Chapter 11
The Freedom Building

My heart was beating wildly as I walked into Theta. All were new girls, and none had a smile for me. It didn't look to me like it would be easy to get along with any.

Mrs. Glenn, the housemother, introduced me to the girls and showed me to my room. All the girls had separate rooms. They were small with one tiny window and about a six-by-eight room. There was just enough room for a twin bed, a chest of drawers, and a tiny closet. The closet had about six hangers, a laundry bag for dirty clothes, and a "honey bucket." I'd never seen a honey bucket before. At JDH and Admittance Cottage, we knocked on our doors if we needed to go to the restroom. There were always housemothers on duty. In St. Rose, we were all in dorms and had access to bathrooms.

It was the newest building on campus, so it had buffed floors. Everything looked clean and shiny. I knew there was no janitor service, so all the girls on the floor did the cleaning.

I opened my room window right away, and the cool spring air rushed in through the metal bars. The sun flashed brightly off the mirror on the chest of drawers.

The girls walked by to their rooms, looking in but saying nothing.

Just before dinner, the girls all lined up at the door to count off, just like JDH had done. One of the girls in front of me turned and introduced herself.

"My names Betty," she smiled. I felt relieved that someone finally spoke. "Why don't you sit by me at the table, and we can get acquainted," she said as Mrs. Glenn unlocked the main door and we walked down the hall to the dining room.

All the girls from all the buildings ate in the same dining room. We were only separated by tables, keeping the groups together from their particular floors and buildings.

Betty had beautiful, long, black hair that she wore in a braided ponytail that I secretly envied. I had always liked long hair, but at that time, I had a long pixie cut.

Betty knew that most of the girls envied her hair and would brush it every night as we watched TV and sling it around when she was on a swing outside. A day wouldn't go by that she wouldn't comment something about it, such as, "My hair's growing," as she looked in the mirror admiringly. "I didn't think it could grow anymore. Do you know what my boyfriend said the last time I saw him? I teased him about cutting my hair, and he said if I did, he'd break up with me," she laughed. "Sometimes I think I just might do it to surprise everyone."

After a few days, the girls began to talk to me. They all wanted to know why I was there and where I was from. I answered all their questions. I missed having a close friend like Donna.

The only other girl who seemed friendly besides Betty was Janet, a colored girl from Salem. She constantly talked about her boyfriend and how he had been sent to prison on a grand larceny charge. "We had the most beautiful rings," she boasted, "and I had them on my fingers when the cops got us. I can actually say I've had 5,000 dollars' worth of rings on my hands at one time."

Later, I saw Donna in the dining room and waved to her. She had been sent to Kappa floor. The only time we could see each other was at the movies on Saturday nights in the gym or in the dining room, where we couldn't speak to each other because our tables were far apart. But on Saturdays, we could get messages back and forth before the movie started. We had to sit in sections with only the people who were on our floor.

That Tuesday, Mother and Barbara came to visit. It was during school again and made me happy to be able to escape school, even though I was keeping my grades above average.

I found that Mother had great news. She said, "Your father and I have consented to let you write to Harley."

I was thrilled and couldn't wait to see my counselor and maybe she'd let me write right away.

Then she added, "Your counselor said she will need three-character references on him, and she will write him with that news shortly."

After our visit, I felt so good hearing I could write him that I was in a super good mood but expected things to go much faster than it did.

The following Tuesday was my sixteenth birthday. I was surprised that Mother and Barb showed up with a cake that said, "Happy Birthday," on it. Barb gave me a stuffed dog, and Mother gave me a pink, checkered, ruffled blouse. I was pleased, but the thought of spending my sixteenth birthday in detention, when I'd dreamed of how it could have been made me feel depressed. I wondered how I'd tell my children someday of how I spent my sixteenth birthday, knowing that particular birthday seemed to be an important one to most people.

Mrs. Glenn had told the girls it was my birthday, and when I returned to the floor from my visit, the girls sang happy birthday and gave me a card that had been signed by everyone on the floor.

"I have some good news for you and a nice birthday present too," Mrs. Glenn said with a smile, putting her arm on my shoulder. "Tomorrow, you'll be transferred to Scott Two."

Some of the girls glared at me. Some had been there for months and had not been transferred, while I had only spent a short time of two weeks on the floor.

"The housemothers had a meeting with the superintendent and Mrs. Snider," she said, "and decided you were ready for more responsibilities and freedom."

I was thrilled.

I wrote a letter to Mother the next day, telling her the good news, and asked her if Barb and her could **please** come the following Sunday because I would be able to leave the campus. I just had to be back by 7:00 p.m.

I liked Scott building, including Mrs. James, the housemother. I shared a room with Martha, an eighteen-year-old girl. Martha was out of school and worked at Fairview. She didn't keep her part of the room very clean, so when the housemothers inspected our room, we got D grades. Martha and I only saw each other in the evenings when we were in our rooms. She was released to go home two weeks later, and I had the room to myself. I kept my room clean and from then on got A's on my housekeeping.

One day, someone brought in a floor buffer machine. I used it in the hall and my room. It took me several minutes to learn how to control it. It was fun, and we all got some good laughs watching each other learn how to control it.

With Scott being the freedom building, we were able to leave our doors open at all times and use the bathroom any time we needed.

I became a close friend of Sandy, whose room was across the hall from mine. When lights were out, we'd lie on the floor and talk quietly across the hall, sometimes giggling about things that happened during the day. Our rooms were the farthest from the office, but we still had to be very quiet so we wouldn't get LPs for visiting after lights were out. The bathroom was across the hall from my room and next to Sandy's.

I felt the few months I'd spent in Hillcrest was constantly meeting new girls and trying to be accepted. I noticed that the girls seemed to be friendlier on Scott than they had been on Theta. I thought the reason for that was the freedom we were given. We were allowed to go out a few afternoons with an elected housemother to nearby baseball games. Once, we were taken to a circus in Salem at the state fairgrounds. We went swimming at Fairview once a week where they had a big indoor swimming pool.

That Friday after school, Mrs. Snider called for me to come to her office. For the first time since I'd been there, I was able to walk out the door, onto the campus, and over to the counseling building instead of walking through the underground tunnel. It gave me a good feeling, and I almost forgot I was in detention.

Mrs. Snider had received a letter from Harley with his selections of three-character references and their addresses. She said she would have to write to each one of them and get their replies. Then when she got their replies, she'd take the letters to the meeting with the superintendent and let her make the decision to accept or not.

"I'll get the letters out this week, and then it depends on how fast they answer," she smiled.

At that moment, I was on top of the world. I felt like I was living again. I just kept thinking how long all this was taking and wished everyone would hurry up.

There were twenty girls on Scott Two floor. Among them were two pregnant girls, Linda and Jackie. Jackie was eight months along. She was extremely quiet and always having conferences with the housemother. I knew she must have been frightened, only sixteen, and having her first baby. She would be adopting it out. Even though she was pregnant, she was given chores.

I hadn't heard from Mother, and when Sunday came, I sat nervously in the day room, waiting and hoping she had received my letter and would take me off-campus. It had been five months since I'd walked down the street, a free person, going wherever I wanted. At that moment, what I thought would be fun was to go to a restaurant and have a hamburger and fries.

The office phone rang. It was the superintendent saying Mother was there, and for me to meet them at her office. I excitably ran down the stairs and across the campus to the main office. I wore my white pleated skirt and the new pink blouse Mother had given me for my birthday. My hair had grown long enough to pull back and wear in a French roll. I signed the register stating I'd be out for the day, and Barb asked me where I wanted to go.

When I told her a restaurant, she laughed! "I never thought that's what you'd say."

I enjoyed my hamburger and fries. Barb had her favorite breaded veal cutlets, and Mother had the same.

After eating, we went to a park nearby. I asked for a cigarette, and to my surprise, Mother gave me one. It made me dizzy, but I didn't let on so she would give another.

The day went all too fast, and it was time to take me back. I begged for them to come see me the following Sunday. Mother insisted it was too far to drive once a week and that I should write Pop and see if he could come.

"He's been so lonesome since Mom has died," she said.

"I'll write him," I said, "but if he can't come, will you, PLEASE?"

Barb spoke up, "If he can't come, I'll come."

Mother grabbed my hand and said, "Your father wanted me to tell you he misses you. Is there anything you want to tell him?"

"Tell him hi for me, okay?"

I hugged them both goodbye at the office, signed myself back in, and went back to my room. Just then, Mrs. James came in and said she needed to search me since I'd gone off-campus. I had no idea I was going to be searched. I had tucked a cigarette in my French roll and felt panic. I stood there waiting to see what the procedure would be. She searched under my bra line and put her hand in my hair, but the cigarette didn't fall out.

About every ten days, we had to stand naked in front of one of the housemothers while they checked our bodies to see if we had put any tattoos on ourselves or for any other new markings. It was an embarrassing situation. I did have a new bruise once, and it was thoroughly examined and recorded.

After she searched me, I went to the bathroom and flushed the cigarette. I was so nervous she was going to find it. It wasn't worth getting into trouble since everything was going so well for me. We were not allowed to smoke. The girls that were eighteen could smoke in her office once a day if they wanted but only in the office with housemothers.

One evening, I walked into the laundry room with shampoo and a towel. I turned on the light and, to my surprise, there were two girls in the corner kissing. It shocked me, and I stared uncontrollably. I had heard about some girls kissing but hadn't seen it. One of the girls laughed, probably because of the look on my face.

"Do you want to see what it's like?" she said.

"No thanks," I said, still shocked. "I just want to wash my hair."

They both continued.

Mrs. James checked the laundry room often because she knew what went on. When she caught girls kissing, they were locked in their rooms for twenty-four hours. They were not allowed out for meals; trays were taken to them. They were probably given honey pots.

If caught a second time, they were sent back to the original floors they were on before they entered Scott building.

As the girls left the room, the one walked up to me and gave me a quick kiss. She laughed and said, "I just wanted you to know what it's like."

I wrote to Pop telling him the wonderful news about my Sundays and asked if he'd consider coming after me.

All week after school, I took a blanket outside and sat on the grass in the mid-May sun. The trees were full of leaves, and the rose bushes bloomed in beautiful pinks and reds. I picked one of the pink roses and was stuck by a thorn under my fingernail. We weren't supposed to pick them, so I figured it was my punishment for disobeying.

Two more weeks, and school would be out. After a short break, summer school would start up, and I knew I would have to go to pass my sophomore year. I didn't mind school much; my subjects seemed easy enough. The only subject that threw me off was modern dance. When I signed up for it as an elective, I didn't realize that modern dance was ballet. I was expecting rock and roll, dancing to the beat of the latest Elvis Presley records instead of Bock and Copán. I hated the outfits we had to wear while we floated gracefully (tried to) around the room. They flattened my bust, and I didn't have much to be proud of at that time.

Saturday, I got a letter from Mother saying she had called Pop, and he had agreed to come see me on Sunday.

That night at the movie, I noticed Donna wasn't in the assembly. I smiled to myself thinking they must have released her to go home. The movie that night was *The Chartreuse Caboose*. Some of the housemothers were offended about the movie because it was about a young couple running away and hiding in a caboose. All the girls were oohing and awing and excited about the choice.

After my chores Sunday morning, I took a blanket outside and watched for Pop's car. He didn't show up until after two, and I was almost in tears thinking he wasn't going to make it.

When I saw him drive up, I hollered and waved and ran up to my floor to wait for the call from the office. When the phone rang, Mrs. James told one of the other girls that her dad was there to pick her up.

When the phone rang the second time, it was for me. I ran down the stairs and over to sign myself out at the main office.

Pop looked tired and had lost some weight. He had weighed about 210, which was about right for his six-foot frame, but he had gone down to 180, which made him look thin.

"How have you been," I asked, trying to be pleasant.

"Well, now that I'm a bachelor and have to run the farm by myself, take care of the trailer park, and do my own cooking, I'm tired and in bed by 7:00 p.m. The dishes are piled to the ceiling, and the dog won't stay home anymore," he tried to laugh.

We took a drive out in the country and stopped at a park to chat and get a little relief from the hot sun. We both laughed at the squirrels running and chasing each other all over the fir trees. Round and round they'd go, chirping and flapping their huge fluffy tails.

We sat by the pond and watched the ducks swimming peacefully. We were both quiet, not knowing what to say. A sad look was on his face as he told me what happened to Mom.

"You know," he began, "when Mom became sick, I took her to the doctor. She kept mentioning the will we had made out together. It was as if she knew she was going to die. That was a couple of weeks before the operation." Then his eyes filled with tears.

He continued, "When the hospital called, it was 3:00 in the morning. All they said was to come to the hospital right away. As soon as they said that, I knew she was gone." He reached for his hanky.

I said, "Please don't cry," as I had tears myself.

We watched the ducks awhile longer and then decided to take another drive. After a few minutes of silence, we felt better and stopped at a restaurant.

While driving back to Hillcrest, Pop began singing an old song I remembered he used to sing when I was very young. I joined in, and after a few minutes, we were laughing.

That Wednesday, when I had some spare time after studying for my exams, I wrote Mother, asking her to come that Sunday. I took a blanket out on the campus and studied till dinner call, then returned to gather my thoughts and relax.

The sky was pale blue and the air so still and warm. The grass was always cut on Wednesdays, and it was one of my favorite smells. I rubbed my hand across a small batch of grass and picked one strand to chew. I didn't notice the sweet taste; my mind was thousands of miles away, wondering what Harley was doing and how he was. I wondered if he would find another girl, he was more interested in.

On Thursday, I wrote a note to Mrs. Snider, asking to see her. The following day, after school, I was asked to the counseling building. I wanted to know about the character references. Mrs. Snider smiled and said not to be impatient. She assured me as soon as she got a letter, she'd let me know.

That Sunday, Barb came to pick me up for the day. Mother wasn't with her. It was only noon, but the sun blazed hot. She brought some hot dogs, so we drove to a park about twenty miles away and ate them. We threw out a blanket and lay in the sun. She told me about her new boyfriend, Dick, and they were going to try out his new motorcycle that evening. She explained she had to take me back early so she could meet up with him at the specific time.

We drove around the country for a few hours smoking, with rock and roll blasting from the radio, enjoying those hot summer days.

When I got back, Jackie had been taken to the hospital. She was gone for a few days and had her baby.

Summer was in full swing, and Pop came to see me and took me to Dexter. He worked on the property driving his tractor, and I rode Cindy. I didn't want to leave; I had enjoyed the horses so much and Tuffy the dog. I talked to Sherry, the girl I had been friends with before we left the trailer park, when Mother divorced Harry. I told her all that had happened since we left the trailer park and where I was living in Salem. She said I could run away at that moment, and she would bring me food. I told her I was sure I only had a few months left there, and it would be really stupid of me to run now.

"Besides," I said, "where could I stay that no one would find me?" She mentioned the dump, where no one went there much. I actually considered it for a few minutes, but then said, "No, I won't take a chance of ruining things."

We had a good chat, rode the horses, and said we'd stay in touch somehow. We had found a place to hide and smoke when I lived there before. She had taken some cigarettes out of her mom's purse, and we rode the horses to the far part of the property and smoked. Pop was busy, and I was sure he didn't see us back in the trees.

It was such a good visit to go to Dexter but a long drive for Pop to come get me, take me to Dexter to ride my horse, take me back to Hillcrest, and then return back to Dexter. So, he only did it once.

Strawberry-picking season started, and some of the girls wanted to go. I wanted to go bean picking, but we weren't allowed because they could not keep a good watch on us like they could in a strawberry field.

They took us to the field in a white state bus. We were all dressed alike in our baggy blue jeans and huge, oversized blue prison shirts. We were only there about four hours, and we had to pick a certain amount, or we would not be able to return for another day.

There was an outhouse that we could walk to. We could go there in pairs. Someone had gotten a cigarette from somewhere and left it in the outhouse with a book of matches. It was pretty well smoked by the time I got there, but I lit it up and got a few drags off of it. We walked down the road with bare feet leaving tracks in the deep powdery dirt. The Maclaren School for Boys was picking in the next field. I looked for a familiar face but didn't see one.

On the way back to Hillcrest, the driver stopped at a convenient store and bought us all bottles of pop. One of the girls could open them with her teeth, so instead of waiting for the bottle opener, several of us girls let her open ours, until the housemother stopped her. It was very hot, so we had all the windows down. We proceeded to drink pop and sing "Ninety-Nine Bottles of Beer on the Wall." We actually had fun, and we were not told to stop singing from the bus driver or the housemother.

A few weeks later, the girls that wanted to and were approved went on a week hike near Mount Hood. Several of us went. We were supplied with donkeys carrying tents and supplies. We each had a backpack with our sleeping bag, cups, water bottles, and utensils. It was not an easy hike; there were many blisters and sore legs and backs. There were about three to six girls in a group, and we each had a counselor for a group.

They gave us material to hand-stitch a flag for our team, any kind of a flag we wanted. We were told about halfway through that the boys from a detention home had been taken the same route a couple of weeks before, and they had complained more about the hike than us girls. If we had wanted to quit, after hearing that, we pressed on. We had to make sure we did better than the boys. It was so hot I walked in one of the streams that flowed from the mountains, onto the trail to cool down my hot feet. I didn't know that was the worst thing to do. I got some pretty big blisters from my leather shoes rubbing my heels.

On one of the log roads, a truck driver with a load of logs stopped as we were crossing. He asked if he could be of any help. One of the girls asked if he had some cigarettes he could spare. He gave her a pack, and she shared with some of the others.

One of the areas we encountered on the way was to either walk through a wide swift stream or cross over on a chairlift, one at a time over the rocks and stream below. The counselor said this would separate the women from the girls. One at a time, the ones who chose the chairlift lined up to take their turn. I used the chairlift, and Sandy chose to walk through the swift stream.

When we arrived at Frog Lake, we found a place to sleep and quickly swept our area with a branch we found from a fir tree. We wanted to make our little spot clean to impress our counselor. We fixed up some dehydrated food for dinner, and since we were all pretty tired from the hike, we crawled into our sleeping bags till morning. We quietly whispered to each other until we were told to get to sleep.

Each night, we had a campfire, and each group presented their flag. There were about ten groups. We all sang and told old and new stories. They had brought one horse along on the trip, and we all got to ride at some point. One night as we were singing, we heard a big crash behind us. We all screamed, thinking it was a bear. After nothing appeared, we all laughed.

The last afternoon we were there, a helicopter flew over the lake and dropped a big bundle. Several girls went out to fetch it. It had been brought in on purpose for us. There were fresh steaks and chocolate ice cream for everyone. We all celebrated the wonderful meal, happy not to eat dehydrated food again that evening.

The following morning, we prepared to leave, getting our backpacks ready to carry down the long dirt trail we came up.

Sandy and I were washing up our utensils at the lake. She was angry about something and flipped some water in my face on purpose. I reacted without thinking. I threw everything I had in my hands in the air and jumped on her. We rolled around in the rocks and dirt, pulling hair and yelling. Some of the girls surrounded us, laughing, then pulled us apart. They gave us each a cigarette and suggested we make up. Our counselor was surprised because Sandy and I were best friends. She also told us if there was another outbreak of that sort, we would go to TW when we got back.

Whatever our problem was, we came to grips and reconciled.

After the long hike back to the bus, we were best of friends again and sat together till reaching Hillcrest.

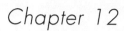

Chapter 12
Don't Turn Around

The days slipped by, I passed the exams, and school was out. That Sunday, Barbara took me home for the day to celebrate. It was a long drive for her to go back and forth from Salem to Portland.

It had been six long months since I'd been home. Everything had changed so much. Barbara had the bedroom painted a different color, and the beds had new white bedspreads on them with our whole collection of stuffed animals placed neatly on top. She wasn't living there anymore, but had fixed the room up for me.

For the first fifteen minutes, all I did was look around without a word.

"I'm glad your home," Harry said from his chair, smiling as he lit up a cigarette.

I believed he meant what he said, that he was glad I was home. All the words Mother had relayed to me about his messages didn't seem realistic until I heard him say them himself and looked him in the face.

Harry looked thin sitting in that big easy chair. He didn't leave that chair much. He had a plugged-in coffee pot on the side table next to him with a bottle of water and a jar of instant coffee. His urinal was on the other side of his chair out of sight. He had a big ashtray and a couple of packs of cigarettes sitting next to his phone. His crutch was within arm's reach to use when he wanted. He also had a remote control for the TV.

Harry rarely sat at the table to eat anymore; Mother brought him meals to his chair. It was very difficult for him to walk. The doctors gave him valium, and he had a prescription for pain. Mother would tease him and say, "Take a tranquilizer; you're making me nervous."

I could see for myself he was not able to travel or get around well.

"I'm glad to be home," I said, "and will be glad when it's for good."

"We will too," Harry said.

I felt uneasy, and none of us knew what to say, so I asked if I could make a phone call to Sue. To my surprise, they said yes, so I called Sue. She was home, and I was so glad to get the connection. I explained to her where I had been for the last several months and that I should be out soon.

It felt like so much time had passed and so much had happened that I even felt uncomfortable talking to her. It was like our friendship had elapsed.

After talking to Sue, I asked if I could visit Linda next door. Linda and I had been friends for so many years that I just wanted to see if she was going to be glad to see me. To my surprise, again, they said yes.

I went next door and visited Linda for about an hour. She seemed glad to see me and had all kinds of questions about Hillcrest. She said Mother wouldn't tell any of the kids where I was, so no one was able to write or ask how I was. She had just told them I wouldn't be back for some time.

I went back to my house, and Mother had dinner ready. We all sat at the table, and Mother teased Barbara about having so many boyfriends.

I watched Harry walk slowly back to his chair, dragging his feet with his wobbling crutch. He had one hand on the wall to help steady himself and almost collapse in his chair when he got close to it.

Mother said she always worried about him falling, as she would have to call someone to help get him to his chair since she was unable to lift him. He was still drinking some, and when he had a few, he would tell her he was going to walk with the invisible rope in the air in front of him. I guess that was a way for him to show off, and after a few drinks, he had courage to do it. I hadn't realized he was so bad and then understood why he hadn't come to visit me.

I didn't feel sorry for him. I really didn't think about my feelings concerning him. I was just glad I was able to make the visit and that Linda, now knowing the truth, could let the kids know all about my disappearance.

When it was time to leave, I hugged Mother, smiled, said goodbye to Harry, and leaned over and gave him a quick hug in his chair. Barbara and I walked out to her car, and, to my surprise, Harry, managed to get himself to the doorway and wave goodbye.

Two weeks later, Mrs. Snider had received two of the three-character references on Harley. I was pleased and prayed for the other one to show up soon, but it never did.

A week later, Mrs. Snider called me to her office. I was sure she had gotten that last character reference. She told me she had not received it yet and that I may have to stay a few more months in Hillcrest. I was surprised as I was sure I was able to go home soon. She said the superintendent and counselor would be having another meeting soon and she would know for sure then.

I went to my room and hit my metal bed with my doubled-up fist. I hurt my hand and left a dent in the headboard. Then I grabbed the curtain and yanked it down, breaking the wooden rod in two.

Right at that moment, the housemother walked up to my open door and said she had good news for me. She looked at the broken rod and curtain hanging there but didn't say anything about it. Then she said, "Your counselor called and said you'll be going home next week." She was testing you to see if you were going to throw a fit, and since you didn't, you passed the test and are going home."

She hadn't noticed the dent in the headboard. I told her I needed a new curtain rod, and she said she'd get me one. I don't know what she was thinking as she looked at the curtains. She didn't say anymore and gave me a new rod.

Sometimes I didn't know why I reacted the way I did. Emotions and reactions that came out even surprised me. Yes, I was disappointed about the six months that I was originally told I would only have to be there if I was good. Then when I was so close to being discharged, they were not sure if I could leave. I thought I had been on the best behavior that was possible for me. As I had such distrust in adults from my past, I had found it hard to trust much from them. I refrained from the excitement of my release because I didn't want to get my hopes up only to have them crushed.

On Tuesday, August 28, I walked to the superintendent's office to sign my release papers. A voice from one of the Patterson's windows said, "You going home?"

I was so excited to say yes until I looked up and saw it was Donna. My happiness quickly turned to sadness.

"Donna, I thought you went home a few months ago. What happened?" I asked.

"Things, just things," she quietly said. "Be good." Then she walked away from the window.

I don't know what she did, but I knew it had to have been bad to end up in Patterson. Maybe she tried to run away; my mind tried to figure out what she might have done. I was unable to ask her any more questions. The girls on Scott Two had told me that when I left, not to turn around and look at the campus, because if I did, I'd return.

Mother and Barbara came after me, and as we left the campus, I felt a strong urge to turn around and take one last look. The reassuring smile from Mother gave me a never-returning feeling, and I looked over my shoulder, and through misty eyes, I watched the buildings fade in the distance.

It's over, I thought, sighing a relief. *This mess is all over.*

Chapter 13
The Marriage I Dreamed About

I had one week to settle in and prepare for the new school year. I signed up at Franklin High. I was so nervous I missed my second class, which was history. I walked the halls and tried to find all my classes so I would know the next day where everything was. I did find the history class but didn't want to go in after class had started, so I just skipped it that day. I managed to get to all my other classes. The following day, the history teacher asked why I had missed the following day, and I told him I couldn't find the room. He then said, "After an hour, you couldn't find the room." Some of the kids laughed, and I was so embarrassed I had no answer to tell him. All I could think of was how much I hated school and thought how rude the teacher was to embarrass me in front of the class.

I met Charlene in the cafeteria, and we became fast friends. Her mother was divorced, and she had one younger sister. We both hated school and would skip classes together. Sometimes we would go to her house because no one was home during the day. Her mother worked in downtown Portland and took the bus every morning to her job. Her younger sister went to the grade school nearby. We could not go to my house because Harry was there most of the time. If he did happen to leave, there would be no way for me to know. Sometimes the school would call parents if their child didn't show up for school. The only way to keep my parents from getting that call was to call them. I'd call and hang up, not saying a word. I'd call three or four times and hang up until they were disgusted with the calls and kept the receiver off the hook. They never did figure it out.

That October, Charlene and I missed several days of school except for a couple of classes we liked. I would go to my English, science, and math classes. Usually, I showed up at study hall and learned how to play, sink my battleship, with the guy in front of my desk and the guy beside me. In math class when I got there, I would ask the guy behind me for all the answers to hand in my homework. He'd just laugh and give me his answers.

My science teacher was involved with studying and helping MS patients, which I didn't know until later. I always pulled good grades in his class. When we studied weather conditions and had to write reports, I always included drawings, explaining my answers. I usually got A's in his class. That was the only class Charlene and I had together, and the next period was lunch, so we would usually leave the schoolgrounds. We walked many times to the McDonald's not far away and ordered the usual, hamburgers and fries, and smoked a few cigarettes.

On Friday, November 12, there was a Columbus Day storm that did major damage to Portland and other areas, with winds over one hundred miles an hour. Charlene and I had been at school, and we left to go to my house. I had an umbrella, and the wind blew it inside out as we walked. Power lines were falling, and when they hit the ground, they flashed with sparks. Several trees had fallen everywhere. We quickly got to my house, and the lights were out. Harry was sitting in his chair with a flashlight. It was still light outside. Mother was at work. Charlene and I wanted to go outside and see all that was happening. We told Harry we were going to go to the movies, and he said okay. He didn't say anything other than to be careful. The movies weren't open because they had no electricity either. The electricity came back on a few hours later in our area. In many other areas, it took up to four and five days. The school had electricity, so it was not canceled.

My cousin Diana and her husband had moved to Portland a few months earlier. On one of the times, we skipped school, I asked Diana to call in the office and say she was my mother and tell them I was ill and wouldn't be there. I told Diana I'd babysit her daughter, Darcy, and she could meet up with her husband and have lunch. She also called and pretended to be Charlene's mother, but the office recognized her voice and knew something was up and called my mother. Since they didn't know where we were, we were not confronted with the "bust" until we showed up at home. The school called my counselor, and she arrived at my house the next day.

She told me I would have to return to Hillcrest if I didn't go back to school because it was the law at that time for anyone under eighteen to be in school. Harry said to me, "If they think they're taking you back to Hillcrest, they can whistle dixie." That really surprised me.

My counselor told me to go to the employment department and get a job. It was either school or a job. That sounded good to me, so I got a live-in babysitting job. The lady had just had a baby and needed someone to care for her two-year-old and help around the house for a few months. I worked for them until the summer ended and my counselor said I had to go back to school or get another job. I went back to school for a while because I was unable to find another job right away, but I had no plans of staying long. Since I was only seventeen and had no driver's license, people felt I was not capable of caring for young children in case there was an emergency.

That November 22, 1963, President John F. Kennedy was assassinated. Some of the kids in school were so frightened, they were crying in the halls. After classes, I walked home, and no one was there. I listened to the news. All that was on the TV and radio was news about the assassination. They showed the swearing in of Lyndon B. Johnson with Jacqueline Kennedy by his side that same day on Air Force One in Dallas. It was a sad day for many. It was dark and rainy in Portland to make it even sadder.

I managed to find another job a couple of months later. That time, I got a live-in babysitting and housekeeping job for a couple, Carl and Pearl, who had adopted a little girl named Carla. They owned two businesses, a laundry mat, and a bar in Portland. They enjoyed hunting and would go hunting with friends and relatives in Eastern Oregon and up the Snake River area. They set up a tent first in Eastern Oregon, where they had a wood stove. They also brought their small travel trailer where Carl and Pearl slept in. A few of us others slept in the tent. Larry, their nephew, brought his four young girls, all under ten, who I didn't know I was going to have to watch. I helped chop wood for the stove and watched all five girls while Larry and the rest went hunting. Fortunately, all the girls behaved surprisingly well.

Pearl did all the cooking in the trailer and handed it out the door for us. One day, Pearl asked me to hunt with her, and the men would stay back and watch the kids. I was pleased to get away from the turmoil for a few hours. I didn't have a hunting license but carried a .22 just in case we had a purpose for it. On the weekend, Larry's wife came, and I was relieved of watching all the kids. I enjoyed hunting, and the weather was nice. A few days later, Pearl came back from hunting carrying a liver and heart. She had filled her tag. Everyone went to help her bring it back to camp.

Pearl, Carla, and I left back to Portland with the deer. She dropped it off at the butchers, and we stayed home for a few days. Carl and friends decided to move their camp and trailer up to the Snake River camp area, where they had had good luck the year before. There were thirteen of us all together.

They parked the travel trailer several miles from town where there was a small camp for hunters to lodge. Then they traveled from there with their jeep, which was a few more miles up the mountain. When

Pearl and I got to the trailer camp in her car, we left her car with the trailer, and Carl picked us up in the jeep and took us to the tent.

Once a week or so, Pearl and I would come down from where we were camped back to Portland and buy food, and she would check on their two businesses. Then we'd return to the tent setup. I enjoyed helping her shop for groceries. There was no budget. Anything we decided we wanted to eat we bought, including lots of candy bars.

Carla was such a sweet little girl. She rarely cried. In the mornings when she woke up, she'd laugh and play with her toys. They dressed her like a little princess with expensive dresses full of ruffles. In the tent, she wore shirts and pants, all matching outfits. Pearl and I took turns washing diapers by hand in a five-gallon bucket with heated water from the stove.

It had been snowing off and on, only a few inches at a time. The temperature was dropping, so we used one tent as storage while we all slept huddled in the tent with the stove. We washed our underwear and hung them to dry in the spare tent. When I went to get mine, they were frozen solid, stiff as a board. That was the only privacy place we had, so Pearl and I had to dress quickly and bear the ice-cold underwear.

One night, there was an unexpected blizzard, and by morning, we were in a desperate way. We had to dig our way out of the tent. We managed to get a station on the small CB we had, and they said the snow drifts had reached in some areas up to twenty feet. One of the young men in our group walked to the trailer lodging area. I wanted to go with him, but Pearl said I'd only slow him down. He and I had gone hunting a few days earlier, and he said he was impressed how I could keep up, for a girl. He managed to get a rescue party to come and bring Pearl, Carla, and me out by horseback.

It was dark by the time we reached the trailer camp lodge. I was on the shortest horse, and sometimes my feet dragged in the snow. Pearl carried Carla on a taller horse. The men in our group stayed behind with the jeep, tents, and all the gear. They wanted to get us women out while it was possible to get out. The three men who came to rescue us went back with us to the trailer lodge. It was a long cold ride, but there was a full moon, and thousands of stars lit the sky, reflecting the trees, casting shadows on the snow. It was so bright it was easy to see the trail the rescuers had made coming after us. We were lucky as it didn't snow anymore that night. I wanted to get down and walk a while because my hands and feet were so cold. One of the rescuer guys gave me his gloves to wear. I think he thought I might have been crying because I had to continue to wipe my cold nose. I wasn't afraid, and the view was like nothing I had ever seen in person. Only in movies and paintings had I seen anything so beautiful.

Pearl and I were so tired when we reached the car. She drove down several of the switchbacks until we reached the closest town. We spent the night at a motel, glad to get warm and have some coffee. We always had baby food snacks for Carla.

That night, we heard on the news that a helicopter had made a rescue for some stranded hunters, and that there had also been a rescue to a party with a baby.

Mother had been listening to the news. She knew that we were all up in that area, and when she heard the news about the rescue of a party with a baby, she believed it was us.

On our way back to Portland the next day, we stopped at the bar where Mother worked and let her know we were safe. That's when she told us she had heard of the rescue. The guys all walked out and left the tents and gear there. They said they'd retrieve it when the weather got better.

We had all been together for a couple of months, and Larry and I seemed to be drawn to each other. Pearl questioned me about it and said, "You don't want to have a Carla, do you?" Then she told me about the affair her husband had with her sister. Her sister got pregnant and had Carla. When Pearl found out, she was extremely hurt but said it wasn't Carla's fault, so she was willing to adopt her. I was shocked and clearly got the message she was saying.

When we were all back in Portland, Carl and Pearl had so many relatives visiting that I felt overwhelmed. Kitchen work was becoming my job, and I felt uneasy about the situation. Several people in the house made me nervous, and Larry was spending the nights there, and the temptation was overwhelming. I loved Harley, but he wasn't there. It had been quite some time since he had been home on leave, and the phone calls weren't often enough. I had to do something before I made a big mistake with Larry. I even liked his wife and wondered what she thought, about him being gone hunting so much and why he was spending nights at Pearl's house instead of going home.

That week, I told Pearl I had to go home and help Mother with Harry, so I quit. I really liked Pearl and adored Carla, so I kept in touch with them off and on by phone for a few years. They had gone back hunting, the following year Pearl said, and Carl had climbed a tree for a better view and fell and broke his neck. He survived to tell his story, and I don't think they went back the following year.

Harley and I wrote and talked on the phone as much as possible. He had been transferred to Andrews's Air Force base in Maryland. He was in search and rescue. We planned to marry when he came home on leave in April.

That Christmas, Harley had sent me an engagement ring through the mail. His family called us, and we all talked about the upcoming event. He was given permission from his commanding officer to get married. I didn't know he had to do that. It seemed odd to me we had to have so many people agree we could marry.

When we picked him up at the airport, I was so excited; we had so much to talk about and important decisions to make. A couple of days later, it was his birthday, and in two weeks, I would have my eighteenth birthday.

We drove two vehicles to Stevenson, Washington. Harley's sister drove us in her car, and Mother and Barb were in the other. We were married there on April 16, 1964. Mother had to sign for me because at that time, one had to be eighteen to get married, and I was still seventeen. We all stopped at a restaurant afterward and ate, then Harley and I used Lucile's car, and they all left back to Portland in Barb's car. Harry didn't go with us, as it was a long way for him to sit in his condition.

The honey moon was a short couple of days, and we returned to Portland, and the family took us to the Portland airport, and we flew to Maryland. Harley's best friend had picked us out an apartment a couple of miles from their house in Washington DC. They picked us up at the airport and took us to our apartment. It was a brick building on the third floor overlooking a wooded area with a nice little brook running through. Rows and rows of brick buildings three stories high. They all looked the same for blocks and blocks.

At that time, the military sent a check to me in my name. It was exactly what the rent was, $123.00. They gave Harley a check in his name as they had always done for $85.00. That's what we lived on for the month. I had saved up some money from working, and it was a good thing. I walked to the office every month to pay the rent, which was about a half-mile down the long street. A couple of times, I had to walk to the office to ask them to come spray the cockroaches and silverfish. I had never experienced those creatures in Oregon, and we had no phone.

We bought a black 1960 Ford Fairlane 500 convertible. It was exactly what his sister had except hers was red. We had enjoyed her car so much that we wanted one like it. The payments were forty-two dollars a month.

We could see the car parking lot from our bedroom. Every night someone would go through all the cars in the parking lot. Some had things stolen, or they ripped up their convertible tops, especially if you locked your car doors. So, we never locked the doors. In the mornings, we would find everything we had in the glove compartment on the front seat. Even my old brownie camera was never stolen.

One of the neighbors had told us if we left the car unlocked, nothing would probably be stolen. Sometimes people would have tires stolen. You never knew what to expect when you went out there. It was a large parking lot to hold vehicles from four apartment buildings. The lighting was sparse for that large of an area.

One night, I saw tiny sparks of light flashing. I'd never seen anything like it before living on the West Coast. They were lightning bugs, also known as fireflies.

The East Coast was so different than the West. It was very humid and warm. We visited everything a sight seer would. I got pictures of the White House, and we walked through the Capitol building, where we were not allowed to take pictures. We walked up the steps of the Washington Monument. I had never seen that many steps in one building; 896 steps the sign read. The windows at the very top were so tiny and old that I could barely see through them. I was worn out from climbing and saw that you could take an elevator down. That suited me. I noticed an older lady walking up the steps with a cane. I had told Harley I was worn out from the climb but felt so embarrassed when I saw her. She had overheard me and smiled.

We weren't going to be living there long, and Harley would be discharged, so I spent several hours a day drawing and didn't look for a job. On days off, we would drive to a park on the Potomac River. We would spend several hours there.

One day, I picked a few little flowers, and a policeman saw me. He told me it was against the law, so I dropped them right there. At that time, Oregon didn't have that kind of law, so I didn't know that it was unlawful to pick flowers in a park. Harley said it was unlawful everywhere in parks, that I just hadn't been caught before.

One day, I went walking through the wooded area by the apartment. I found three turtles the size of my hand and brought them back. I put them in the bathtub and had a good time watching them. I gave them some goodies to eat and things to climb on. I was missing the country. When Harley went to take a shower that night, he was surprised to see the turtles and laughed.

The following day, I took the turtles back to the brook where I found them. I enjoyed that area and walked through it almost every day. It was my "getaway," and it was the only little forest around for several miles.

Sometimes I'd go for long walks that took me a few miles from the apartment. I wasn't afraid, even though some people stared at me like I was out of my area and shouldn't be there. I had a hard time staying cooped up in that building. I was glad we were only going to have to spend a few months there.

Harley had a few friends in the military who came to visit. I didn't care for them much but didn't say anything. We all smoked in those days and drank when we could afford it. We had bought a TV at Sears when we got there, along with a few other household items. Most of our entertainment was from the TV.

One evening, Harley brought home a tiny black puppy. He had it zipped up in his coat. He said, "I have a surprise for you." Someone had talked him into adopting it. I was thrilled to see her and named her Shazon.

The day he was discharged was a cold rainy day in late February. We cleaned up the apartment well so we could get our one-hundred-dollar deposit back. They said they would mail it to us if they were satisfied with the cleaning.

We packed everything we owned in the car. There was very little room for us to sit, and we fixed a little spot for Shazon. We only stopped four times from DC to Oregon for motels, and it was freezing cold all the way there. One of the stops was in Kansas. It was so cold and windy that my face ached. The motel said no cooking or pets. We brought in our electric skillet, and I cooked hamburger and potatoes. We smuggled Shazon in under coats and a blanket. I'm sure the food could be smelled, but no one complained. Shazon was quiet, and we all got a much-needed good night's sleep. She was used to using newspapers that we could find free most everywhere.

The car burned oil, but as long as we kept putting it in, it kept running. Gas was twenty-five cents a gallon. We ate potato chips and cold vegetable soup from the can with crackers and kept driving.

As we rolled into Baker, Oregon, a wheel bearing went out. We had not heard any warning noises because of the wind and rain being so loud on our canvas convertible top. We managed to limp into the first gas station that was open.

It was costly for us, but our destination was only 300 miles away then. We had traveled a long distance and, incredibly, had no major problems. We got a motel, and I cooked, and we brought Shazon in. We found a phone booth and called Mother and told her we were almost there.

We stayed with each family member for a couple of days while searching for a place to rent. The best and cheapest rent, was at the apartment complex where Barb lived west of town overlooking I-5. We weren't to stay long, as we were unable to have pets there, so Mother cared for Shazon till we found a nice little house in Tigard with a fenced yard.

Harley got a job working for Paul Lumber. He was low on the totem pole, so it only lasted a few months. At that time, Shazon had five puppies. We didn't know she was pregnant, but while at Mother's there was a visitor who came by that none of us knew about. All the puppies died except one we named Shan. We took her to the vet, and he said she had acid in her milk and that was the problem. We took Shan in the house and raised him separately. We let them be together every day but wouldn't allow Shan to nurse.

We went to visit Pop as much as we could. I rode Cindy and took some pictures. Harley wasn't really interested in horses, but we spent the day there and had a good time. We went over to the lake and spend the night in the car. We parked at the lower Dexter Dam and fished for catfish and bass. The dogs were able to run around and sniff out exciting things.

Pop had given Tuffy away to a lady we all knew. Tuffy had been shot by a farmer down the road because he was trying to breed with one of his registered dogs. He survived the shot, and the lady, who was a registered nurse, took care of him and took him with her when she moved to Arizona.

Harley wanted to continue fishing, so I walked over to the trailer park. Pop gave me $200.00 for Cindy and said that was my money back for when I sent it to him to buy me a horse. He said I'd probably need it for baby bottles and such. He knew I didn't have a place for her and needed the money.

We talked about the farm. He knew I loved the horses and the cows. I told him he should go on a vacation, visit Hawaii, or something. He said he had everything he wanted right there. He had his favorite rocking chair in the breeze way, outside the back door, and could look at Dexter Lake and enjoy the quiet scenery. It was a perfect spot, and later I'd enjoy that same spot, thinking the same thing. (I have everything I want). He showed me where he had some money hidden in a shoebox in case anything should happen to him. He also said he had money locked up in his car glove compartment.

We went to the local restaurant at the Dexter intersection beside the little country store. We ordered hamburgers and fries, and Pop shook his head about the price of a dollar-twenty-five each. He said when he was young, he could get a hamburger fries and milkshake for five cents. That amazed me.

We left and went back and sat in the rocking chairs in the breezeway. It was a warm day, and there was a gentle breeze. We could see Look Out Point Dam from there through the trees, and I asked him what would happen if the dam broke. He didn't believe it would flood the house he said, but there would be a lot of water all around. We just made small talk, and Harley came and said it was time to go home.

A couple of months later, Pop passed away. It was told to us he fell off his tractor, and someone found him. He had had surgery for cancer about a year prior, but that wasn't the cause of his death.

Mother, Barb, and I drove to Dexter to see what all had to be done and went to the funeral later that afternoon. Sherry, the girl who I had been friends with there at the park, she and her parents came to visit when they heard the news of Pop's death. Pop had given her one of the horses (Fletcher) that she loved so much.

Sherry and I went out to the barn to visit the horses. We sat on a few of them and just talked about all that had happened to us in the last few years since we were riding the horses there last.

I told Mother about the shoebox he had told me about, but it was gone, and the glove compartment in his car had been broken into. There was not a penny found in the house.

Harry Jr. then inherited the property in Dexter. We all drove out there a few days later so he could see everything he had inherited. He enjoyed watching the horses run as we drove through the fields looking at them. He wasn't driving anymore. He didn't seem to be remorseful about Pop. In fact, he seemed to have no special feelings at all. Mother made a joke, saying, "Mom looked down from heaven and grabbed Pop by the ear and said, 'I miss you; come up here.'"

Since Mother hated the country life and Harry couldn't do much of anything anymore, they decided to sell it. That broke my heart. Harry said Harley and I could move into Pop's house and care for the place until it sold. My job there was to care for the cows and horses and collect rent from tenants, and Harley's job was to maintain the area and mow the grass. There was a lot of grass in that trailer park. Trailers had big spaces, and there was a total of about four acres. Only a few people mowed their own yards. Pop always used the tractor to go through the park and mow, but Harry sold the tractor and implements right away, leaving us with the mower I had chopped those roses of Mom's down with.

In the spring, one could spend days mowing and keeping up the grounds, collecting garbage, and so on, and hauling it to the dump. In the fall, the leaves from all the maple trees kept us busy.

Harley's youngest brother Johnny was starting high school and moved in with us. He went to Pleasant Hill High School. He was a big help. We all mowed and raked but were still overwhelmed.

Barb and Mother showed up and helped one weekend, and we managed to get a lot done. We always found time to have fun riding horses up the mountains and camping out. Harley enjoyed the horses more and more, and soon almost as much as me. Johnny went along, usually complaining about his sore butt. We gave him Laura to ride. She was young and clumsy. She was a registered appaloosa I had bought to train and resale. We got a lot of laughs at Johnny's expense. Laura never fell but just tripped a lot.

When we rode to the thirty acres behind the railroad tracks, we packed food, beer, and pop. When we got to our favorite spot, we built a small fire to cook on. Then we'd set up our empty cans and take turns shooting our riffles.

One night at home, we heard Shan continually barking, and we couldn't figure out what was wrong. A couple of hours later, when it was daylight, I saw that Shazon had gotten out of the fence and was lying on the road. I buried her with her toys in the field. She had come into heat and went looking for a mate. We had built a four-foot fence to keep the dogs in, but she was persistent and got out somehow. Shan tried to tell on her, but because it was still dark, we thought he may have been barking at a possum or something.

Some friends down the road who raised German Shepherds felt bad for my loss and said to come and take a pick of their dog's last litter. I picked the shyest one hiding under the bed and named her Mona. She was about three or four months old. They had had the mother bred to a registered German Sheppard from Arizona and were pretty proud of the litter.

One day, Donna stopped in to rent a trailer we had advertised for rent, the trailer that our family had lived in for several years. Oh, I was so happy and surprised to see her. It had been about four years since we had seen each other in Hillcrest. We caught up on old and current news. We visited most every day. She had a little boy about two, with curly black hair and the longest eyelashes I'd ever seen. He was a handful and kept her busy.

I had another friend in the trailer park who was married with two kids. Ruth and I rode together every day in warm months. Her husband, Fred, enjoyed riding also, and Harley and I would take them up the mountains with us sometimes. At that time, they didn't own any horses.

Barb married George that March in 1966. They came to visit us often. They drove a Volkswagen bus and brought their bright-eyed cockapoo puppy they had named Windy Pooh.

We all went riding up the mountain behind the railroad tracks. Then we drove to the coast and bought several crabs to snack on. Crab was thirty-nine cents a pound, and gas had gone up to thirty-one cents a gallon.

We took some trips to Eastern Oregon, and Barb and I and the dogs slept in the Volkswagen, and the husbands slept outside on cots. We could hear the coyotes yipping in the night, and in the morning, it was so cold the windows were fogged over. I rubbed the fog off and looked out the window and saw the frost on our husbands' sleeping bags. We were glad to get up, let the dogs out for a few minutes, and drive to the nearest café for hot coffee. I always hated to see them leave as we had so much fun together wherever we went. They both worked at that time in Portland, so only their weekends were free. We talked about one day driving to Alaska and taking a leisurely month to do it.

I rode in any kind of weather, pouring rain, hot or cold. Every morning, I'd go out to the pasture with a curry comb and brush. I'd brush the horses right out in the field. They were never hard to catch even though I rode every day. Some days I'd take the stallion for a good workout up the hills. He was easygoing and rode well with other horses. I also trained some of the younger horses enough to ride so Harry could sell them, we called them, "green broke".

I couldn't work hard or fast enough for Harry, and he complained a lot, along with his foul mouth. All the complaining he did he had to do by phone or mail. Mother said she ran after the mailman a few times to retrieve some mail Harry had sent out. She said it was so foul she didn't want us to get it. Harry didn't pay us for working for him; he just gave us free rent.

Harley found a job not far away at a lumber mill, and I picked beans, apples, and had a garden. We went hunting and filled our tags. The deer came on the property and grazed along with the cows. We raised some rabbits and chickens and a couple of beef calves.

Harry sold all his cattle to a company in Eastern Oregon. The hundred-acre pasture looked pretty bare after they left. It was dotted with about ten horses, and the grass was so high that spring you could barely see them.

Once in a while, we had to go to Portland to visit, usually on holidays, mostly Christmas. I dreaded it, although it was good to see Harley's relatives and Barb and George. Sometimes Harry would act okay as long as you agreed with him.

I loved the farm, but Harley's job at the mill had ended, and we had to move and look for jobs that could support us. At that time, I had two dogs and three horses. I sold one horse and kept Molly, who I had bought from Harry, and a colt I had bought from a guy in Eugene.

If ever there would have been a perfect life for me, it would have been right there. Riding horses every day and tending the cattle. I felt I would have been happy there for the rest of my life.

I had a 30-30, and Harley had a 30-06. Most of the time, we shot off the horses. After a while, they got used to the noise and stood quietly. Once when I rode Molly up the hill behind the railroad tracks, she stopped and stared into the brush. I strained my eyes and finally saw what she had stopped for. There was a buck standing in the shadows by a tree. I took aim and shot him right in the juggler. He jumped up and fell straight down, and that was it. I had aimed to shoot him behind his ear, but I got him and was happy. We put him on Molly's saddle, tied it down, and walked home. We were still on Pop's property.

I cried the day we left Dexter. I left the farm and the trailer park in the hands of Ruth and Fred. That seemed to be okay with Harry. Harley and I had tried to talk Harry into selling us a four-acre parcel that the homestead was on. He said he thought about it but decided not to.

We were able to keep our horses there until we found a place to rent. We found a small house outside of Portland, and fixed a fence for the dogs and our two horses, on the neighbors' pasture next door. We were there about a year and bought a ten-by-fifty trailer and moved to St. Paul on a lady's farm that had a trailer space for rent.

I sold the colt I had and bought a Welsh/Arabian filly from Garry Warren in Springfield who raised Arabians. I met people who had horses in the area, and we would meet up and ride for miles. Some of the riding was on the paved country roads, but the owners of the hop fields in the area let us ride through on their property.

At that time, I started riding in parades. The parades were quite large, and I was so excited to do what I had dreamed of, and prayed for since I was a child. Sometimes I was awarded a ribbon or trophy, that made me want to enter anytime there was a parade nearby. Harley didn't want to ride the parades, but he helped me prepare for them and drove us there. Barb sewed me a beautiful blue serape for behind the saddle, and I sewed blue and white flowers on it. We went to a Western store and I bought a blue Western suit to wear. Everything matched, and I was having fun.

We moved again to Carlton on a friend's property who let us raise chickens and keep our two horses and a calf. We worked for them doing odd jobs for free rent, and Harley got a job working at the Newberg Mill. We were there about six months and then moved to Newberg on two acres.

His job was only three miles away, and the pay was good. Harry had sold the Dexter property and lent Barb and George money for a twelve-by-sixty trailer. Harry loaned Harley and me money to buy the two acres in Newberg, and we paid him 4-percent interest. We bought a car and sold our ten-by-fifty trailer and bought a used twelve-by-sixty-foot mobile home with two slide outs. To me, that was a beautiful trailer. The step-up kitchen I thought was really fun. We put a fireplace in, and it was quite a nice little home for a trailer. After putting in new woven wire horse fence and a thirty-by-thirty pole barn, we were feeling on top of the world. We bought a used two-horse trailer so we wouldn't have to haul the horses in the back of the truck anymore, now that we had bought a camper.

During summers, we would have a huge garden and give produce to Mother and city friends who weren't so blessed with room for a big garden. Harley enjoyed working in the garden all summer. I didn't like the planting and weeding, but I enjoyed the canning.

We felt we had it all together and enjoyed every weekend doing whatever our hearts' desires were.

I started working as a housekeeper at the local motel in Newberg. We were buying so many toys and enjoying life so much that it was even more then I had dreamed for. Most days, I only worked four or five hours. Eventually, I stopped cleaning rooms and worked some evenings in the office. I made more money, and it was less work.

Some new people moved in at the end of our country road with their trailer and built a large barn with an indoor area. Vic and Steve were in their twenties also and planned to train horses and show professionally. We became good friends, and I watched their three children many times as they combed the country buying horses that they could train and sell for profit. I helped exercise them and cleaned stalls for the privilege of riding my horses in their arena. That was very handy, especially in the rainy months.

I learned so much from them; it helped me later in my own business. They had enough horses to have a riding stable, and people came from all around to ride. She taught classes in 4-H, so I automatically got involved because I was there.

That's where I met Rhoda, whose family and I became close friends. Rhoda was an exceptional rider at thirteen and, over time, became a jockey. She and I spent many hours riding in and around Walker Pond, across the road from Vic and Steve's property. She had a thoroughbred mare and would practice jumping downed rotting trees on the paths or anything jumpable. I rode my Arab/Welsh most of the time following her. Short "Tana," barely measuring fourteen hands, surprised me at the heights she could jump following along behind Rhoda's tall thoroughbred.

They had moved to Oregon from an area near Carmel, California, and had always had a horse for Rhoda. She also had a large pony just a little shorter than Tana she called Buddy. In the warm months when she rode Buddy, we would ride bareback and swim with the horses in Walker's Pond that covered about five acres. Then we'd race them across the huge field beside the pond. Once, Tana slipped and fell, and somehow, I landed on my feet, still holding my boots from the swim.

When Rhoda was in school, I'd go riding with other people who came for lessons or to just take a leisurely ride. I preferred leisurely rides.

Vic encouraged me to start showing Tana at horse shows instead of the parades. Rhoda was all for it and wanted to put her in 4-H. So, Rhoda started riding Tana in 4-H along with her horses. Sometimes we'd have two horse trailers with horses at a show for her to ride in different classes. Harley drove one trailer, and her mother drove another. We were enjoying all the outings with horses, even driving out of state for some events.

I decided I wanted to show and chose Trail Horse Class to go in with Tana. She did so well that the competition hated seeing us arrive at the shows. I also rode her in some Western and English classes. She had quite a reputation of being a horse that anyone could ride, and several people wanted to buy her. My answer was always, "No."

The horse shows, 4-H projects, and work consumed all our time, and we enjoyed every bit of it.

Chapter 14
My Best Decision

We had a friend we had met in Dexter we called Uncle Irv. He rode a BMW motorcycle and had a wooden box fastened on the back for his white poodle mix dog. He rented one of the cabins in Pop's trailer park. He was a senior in his late fifties. He was a quiet and humble guy but loved to travel and would make frequent trips to Reno and gamble. He said he'd just pull over under a tree anywhere and park for the night. One night, there was a rainstorm, and lightning hit the tree close to him. He said that was the last time he slept out under the trees. He bought a Chrysler, and from then on, he and his dog slept in it on their travels and excursions.

In the summers, he'd often visit us. He and Harley's dad became close friends. They were about the same age, and both had lost their wives and never remarried. One of Irv's sons had drowned that year. He was an excellent swimmer but crossed a swift river while fishing with his hip-wading boots on. Onlookers said he went under and came up pulling his boots off, but the second time he went under, he didn't come back up. Irv showed us pictures of him in a casket. He was a young man in his twenties, strong and athletic, and everyone who knew him were surprised of his accidental death.

Dad and Irv spent about two weeks with us, and we had a project we worked on while Harley was at work. We built a new well shed and painted it to match the mobile home. The old one was only three feet high and hard to fix anything when we needed to. That seemed to be more often than we liked.

At that time, I was overwhelmed with the barn chores, my job, and trying to be a good hostess to Dad and Irv. I was tired and exhausted, enough to the point that I went to the doctor.

I was having dizzy spells and used the walls in the mobile home to walk. They took a few blood tests and just couldn't pinpoint the problem. My doctor told me he had checked for everything imaginable except for mononucleosis. He said he didn't check for that because I was twenty-three and that was too old for mono. He said that my blood sugar was extremely low, so he put me on a special diet. I still had problems, so he decided he'd check me for mono, and was surprised to see that I had it. He said it looked like I was having a nervous breakdown along with it. He gave me medications, but it only worsened, so he put me in the hospital for one month in Portland. I was given vitamin shots and tranquilizers.

Harley came to visit me with flowers, and I fell asleep, so he left. Ten days later, I was encouraged to walk and get fresh air outside. Rhoda came with him, and we took a walk in the sunshine, and I began to feel better.

Harley had bought me a small stuffed animal, and I had it beside me in the hospital bed. The last night I was there, I put the toy under my bed to scare the nurse. The nurses had a habit of dropping bed pans in the middle of the night, and I'd hear them giggling, so I thought I'd give them a scary goodbye gift to pay them back. When she came in with her flashlight, as she did every night, she saw it and jumped back. Then she put the flashlight on it again. She didn't say anything, but I knew it startled her. I was awake, waiting for her reaction, and it made me smile.

When I returned home, I began seeing a psychiatrist weekly. It looked like my past life had done damage that was causing the symptoms I was having.

I had some good chats with the doctor, and he gave me medication that was too strong, and I was unable to maneuver around to do my daily chores. He tried several different prescriptions over the weeks, and I hated them all. Nothing was working, in my opinion. He suggested I go to the hospital where I could be monitored to get on a medication that worked. I told him I was unable to do that again because I had animals to care for and needed to work and help with the finances. I was pretty depressed when I got home.

I thought all week about how much work we had done on the property and how happy I was with everything going in my life. I had the husband I wanted and had the horses I'd prayed for since I was two or three years old. We had a nice home; Harley had a good paying job, and I loved having and riding the horses. I was unable to figure out what was wrong, and I wanted to be well.

One afternoon when Harley was at work, I turned on the TV. There was Oral Roberts. I hadn't seen him since Aunt Evelyn and Mother had decided not to put their hand on the TV for prayer. He talked about how important it was to put Christ in your life and to be sure you are saved. So, when you die, and no one knows when that will be, you'd go to heaven. I listened to him intently, and at the end of his program, he said, "If you want to be saved, repeat after me." He reached his hand out to the TV, and I put my hand on the T.V, and prayed to receive Christ as my Savior, and I asked for the forgiveness of sins. Something happened. I thought, *what is this feeling I'm having?* It's something I'd never felt before. It was more than happy; it was joy, and I never wanted to lose it. It was peace, and I wanted to share it.

When I was baptized at ten, I repeated what the pastor said and answered his questions, but I didn't have the feeling I had when I prayed this time. I believe it was because I fully understood what I was saying and hadn't asked for the forgiveness of sins before, because I didn't know that was necessary.

When Harley came home, I told him what had happened. He said, "Well, I don't believe in the Darwin theory." He didn't quite know what to say. I asked him if he'd go to church with me, and he said, "Well," his dad had gone a few times to the Lutheran church, so he would do that.

When I was a child, I went to the church in Dexter in the trailer park, but I didn't know what denomination it was. Then we had attended the Baptist church where I was baptized, and I liked it. As we talked, we decided we'd go to the Lutheran church. I remembered I had a Bible and knew I had it packed away in the trunk I had in the shed. I went out and finally found it after digging through to the bottom. There were two: one I received when I was baptized, and the other was a pretty white Bible that Grandma Rosa had given me years ago. I think she gave Barb and me each one.

That Sunday, Harley and I went to the Lutheran church. We both liked the pastor, and after a few weeks of attending, he came out to visit us.

I decided to read the Bible and started at the beginning like a normal book. I was surprised to see I could understand it, since I had been told in the past that most people don't understand it. The more I read, the more I began to understand. It was the old King James Version. I enjoyed all the stories and had finished reading it in four months.

I was so absorbed in King David that when I finished reading about him, I didn't want the story to end. I wondered why his best friend Jonathan had to die and why King Saul acted the way he did. People in the Bible weren't perfect, yet God managed to work with them for His will to be done.

I had a big smile when I read in Numbers 22:21 through 32, where a donkey talked to Balaam, his master. I realized that God can do anything.

I told Mother and Harry about what had happened to me and brought Mother a book about Jesus. She was happy, but Harry told me to "get out" and don't bring that stuff to their house anymore. Mother kept the book. Harry told me to leave, so I did. I was so shocked to think that he would not be pleased to hear my good news. I wasn't angry at him. I just felt sad.

I told my neighbors, Sherry and Dave, about my salvation. I hadn't realized they were Christians also because they hadn't mentioned it. I told Barb and George, and they were so happy they started going to a church near their place. I wrote a friend I had met in St. Paul, telling her about my experience. She had moved away, and she wrote back, saying, "Something really good did happen to you."

I watched Christian programs on TV and enjoyed writing poetry. I began spending more time drawing that I had enjoyed before, but had put aside while fulfilling my time with horse activities. I took a home Bible course and enjoyed answering the questions that I had to send back to be graded.

Between the new diet, vitamins, and studying God's Word, I felt better and began to get the health back that I had lost.

When I visited Mother and Harry, I didn't talk about Christianity anymore; I just went to visit.

One day, Mother said Harry couldn't find anyone to play cribbage with, and he enjoyed that card game so much. So, I learned how to play cribbage, and we had some laughs. I got pretty good at that game and really enjoyed it. He didn't get upset when he lost, and I was glad to see he could laugh and even smile at times. It had been a long time since I'd seen that side of him.

Harry had a big problem with his teeth, so he had to go to the hospital to have them all pulled. Mother and I went and stayed all day with him.

After the surgery, he tried to talk to the nurse. She couldn't understand him because his mouth was full of cotton to stop the bleeding. I could understand him quite well, and I told her, "He's afraid he's going to fall out of bed, because the MS makes him feel unbalanced." She assured him he wouldn't fall and put several pillows around him. Since she was unable to understand him, he looked at me, and I told her again what he was saying. I saw tears in his eyes. I left the room then and burst into tears. I had never seen him in a pathetic state. I felt sorry for him. I had never felt sorry for that man.

One of the doctors came in with five or six people, stating, "Here's a man with MS." They all wanted to touch his hands and see if he had feeling and asked him some questions. I felt angry and thought they were treating him like he was some kind of freak. I left the room angry and sad for him, and then wondered why I had those feelings.

When he arrived home and was healing well, he got his new teeth. He would take them out and make funny faces, and Mother would tell him to stop. I thought it was so funny that I laughed. He learned to drop the teeth just far enough out of his mouth so they wouldn't fall completely out and clang them together. Mother couldn't seem to stand it, but it was hilarious to me.

We had Christmas dinners there, and the neighbors, Bunny and the family, came over. On Thanksgiving, we were invited over to Bunny's house for dinner. All the kids were grown and married, and some had children. Barb and George had two children, Kari, the firstborn, in 1970, and Michael in 1971.

Harry went to the hospital on June 11, 1976, which happened to be Mother and his anniversary. Harley, George, Barb, and Mother went to the hospital. Harley called me and said, "If you want to see him alive, you need to come to the hospital now."

I said, "No, that's okay." He said he had asked Harry if he wanted to send Mother anniversary flowers but got no response, and said he was incoherent and in anguish. That's why I decided not to go see him. Barb said he was physically thrashing in the hospital bed.

He passed away that day and was cremated and put in a vault, where, when Mother's time came, she would be put in the same vault.

There were more people at the wake than I expected. I wondered what life would be like for Mother as she proceeded on her journey alone, as they had been married twenty-eight years.

I visited Mother often, and we watched Christian TV and prayed when they prayed. We had special ones we enjoyed, and I'd call for prayer sometimes.

Shortly after that, Barb guided her through the process of salvation. Mother told me how excited she was and went through her house and removed things she felt displeased God, like the Buddha statue she had brought back from overseas, when she had visited Uncle Russ. She didn't worship the idol, although she had rubbed his tummy in fun.

That Christmas, she sent cards and wrote to several relatives and friends stating that she had accepted Jesus as her Savior.

I don't know what happened to Harry. Did he go to heaven? He knew about God, and I'm sure Mother prayed for him. One day, as we were talking, he said he knew what was in the Bible and even told me one of the stories. I just listened. I was shocked he brought it up and troubled about the story he chose. I just listened and nodded because the story is in the Bible. At least he was thinking about God's Word.

What happened to him in his life that made him like he was? He seemed to like to talk about his mischievous past in the Navy and a little about his teenage years. He didn't talk about his young life at home, his parents or teachers, or even the chores he had on their pig farm in Denver. He did like animals and had a soft spot for stray dogs. One of his favorite sayings were, "Marry an orphan and move to Alaska." He didn't like many people around and said relatives were a nuisance.

He did have a strong influence on my childhood that I feel kept me from some potentials I could have had. I wondered what caused him to be so belligerent in the Navy that he forfeited an honorable discharge. Did some horrible things happen to him that he didn't recover from? Could one of his parents been the cause of his outrageous temper? Did he learn as a child that a bad temper could result in getting his way? Had my behavior been a copy of his? It can only be speculated and not known.

When a person is dying, I believe they cry out to God. I have to believe that a person has that last chance.

Wherever you are, Harry, I forgive you.

Only God knows the heart, so we won't know who all will be in heaven until we get there. We just pray they will be.

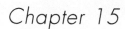

Chapter 15
Antics of Harry, Mothers Childhood

Harry Jr. was born in Denver, Colorado, on October 1, 1921. His parents, Harry Sr. (Pop) and Rosa (Mom), lived on a farm there and raised pigs. Harry Jr. relayed that he was quite a prankster in his youth.

He didn't reminisce much about his childhood. He said they were poor, and he could remember having to eat a pig that had died on the farm, and they didn't know how it had died.

I don't recall him saying he had any particular hobbies. He did say that men should be interested in sports. He liked to watch the World Series baseball games on television in later years.

Harry stated he hated his father but loved his mother. He liked most animals, especially dogs. He loved fried foods, especially pork chops and fried potatoes.

They left Denver and moved to Cascade Locks, Oregon, where he acquired a liking for dynamite, and he and his teenage friends would set some off in areas to scare people.

Once, he set one off in an outhouse. No one was in the outhouse; he said that they wanted to know what it would do to the building. He said it didn't totally destroy it.

One Halloween, he and his friend took a pair of jeans and a shirt, stuffed them full of hay, and laid them on the road late at night. They hid behind some bushes not too far away and watched traffic stop and check it out, probably thinking it could be a hurt or dead man on the road.

One night, he and a friend "borrowed" a neighbor's donkey and put him in the principal's office at school. They closed the door and fed the donkey Ex-Lax. He said that no one ever found out who the pranksters were.

He was in WWII in the Navy. He was on the ship "Hawaiian." He said they were attacked, and a guy standing next to him was killed, and he was wounded.

He liked to party and drink.

One day, his sergeant in the military angered him for something he said. Harry said he would knock his but off, and the sergeant laughed and said, "You can't hit me because I'm an officer." So, Harry hit him. Then he was in the brig for several weeks and received a dishonorable discharge. (That cost him dearly in later years).

Mother said when they got married, she had to wake him up with a broom handle because he would jump up swinging and fighting, thinking he was still at war.

I don't know why he had such a dislike for his father. Once, Pop told me a story of when he was young about his uncle and cousins, who had wrestled him down and forced him to drink alcohol and poured it all over him. So, Harry Senior had a hate for alcohol. He didn't chew or smoke.

No one knows why people do the things they do. I believe we are a product of our upbringing. If parents are dysfunctional, no doubt their children will be. Disease and mental illness, either living with it personally, or living amongst it, plays a role also. Choosing friends wisely is a benefit that lasts a lifetime.

I don't recall Harry Jr. saying he went to church as a child or teen.

Yet, his mother taught Barb and me how to say the Lord's Prayer.

I'm sure she prayed for him, and had mentioned attending church.

Mom and Harry Jr.

***Harry Jr. in front of Mom's Beloved Roses
Dexter***

Mother's Childhood

Doris was born in 1923. She loved her mother, Rosa, and father, Fritz, although she was closest to her father. Her mother divorced Fritz and moved to Oregon to be close to some family. Mother stayed with her father for a few years.

Evelyn was the firstborn, then Russ. Mother was born nine years later.

As a child, she lived mostly in the city with all the connivances that were available at the time. Since Russ and Evelyn were much older than her, they moved and were out on their own in Oregon. Evelyn had been born with a cleft pallet and accused her mother as the reason for it.

Mother said one day, Evelyn chased Rosa around the house with a knife because of her lip. She had surgery correction as a young child but didn't like the end result. There were very few pictures taken of Evelyn in her lifetime, and of those pictures, she held her hand in front of her face.

Rosa sent Mother to a Catholic boarding school when she was around ten. She really liked the school and had a boyfriend there (puppy love). She said they would sneak out of their rooms at night and meet up. I don't know how long she was there.

When she met Roger, my dad, they fell in love and decided to drive to Arizona to get married. It was a short marriage, and they divorced right after the war (1946) after Barb and I were born.

Mother didn't like the country but loved the cities with excitement and bright lights.

Mother loved to wear pretty dresses and heels and have her hair done. She fixed her long red hair for years until later when she married Harry, she went to hairdressers.

Mother's appearance was very important to her, and you could smell her perfume when she walked in the door. It was nice but strong. She turned the eyes of many men, which I believe brought trouble to both her marriages.

Grandma Rosa, Fritz, Evelyn and Russ

Mother 1937
S. Dakota

Russ with Kayo Erickson, (a cousin) that had a part in the movie, as a Munchkin, in "The Wizard of Oz"

CPSIA information can be obtained
at www.ICGtesting.com
Printed in the USA
BVHW032118170722
642308BV00020B/177